BELL'S CATHEDRAL SERIES:
EDITED BY GLEESON WHITE
AND EDWARD F. STRANGE

LICHFIELD

Photochrom Co. Ltd., Photo.]

LICHFIELD CATHEDRAL FROM THE WEST.

THE CATHEDRAL CHURCH OF
LICHFIELD
A DESCRIPTION OF ITS FABRIC
AND A BRIEF HISTORY OF THE
EPISCOPAL SEE

BY

A. B. CLIFTON

WITH THIRTY-NINE 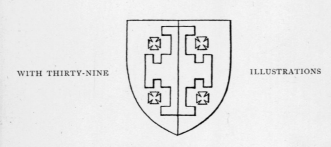 ILLUSTRATIONS

LONDON   GEORGE BELL & SONS   1898

3-12869 1/2

W. H. WHITE AND CO. LIMITED
RIVERSIDE PRESS, EDINBURGH

GENERAL PREFACE

THIS series of monographs has been planned to supply visitors to the great English Cathedrals with accurate and well illustrated guide-books at a popular price. The aim of each writer has been to produce a work compiled with sufficient knowledge and scholarship to be of value to the student of Archæology and History, and yet not too technical in language for the use of an ordinary visitor or tourist.

To specify all the authorities which have been made use of in each case would be difficult and tedious in this place. But amongst the general sources of information which have been almost invariably found useful are :—(1) the great county histories, the value of which, especially in questions of genealogy and local records, is generally recognised ; (2) the numerous papers by experts which appear from time to time in the Transactions of the Antiquarian and Archæological Societies ; (3) the important documents made accessible in the series issued by the Master of the Rolls ; (4) the well-known works of Britton and Willis on the English Cathedrals ; and (5) the very excellent series of Handbooks to the Cathedrals originated by the late Mr John Murray ; to which the reader may in most cases be referred for fuller detail, especially in reference to the histories of the respective sees.

GLEESON WHITE,
EDWARD E. F. STRANGE,
Editors of the Series.

AUTHOR'S PREFACE

CONCERNING any old Cathedral the mass of information is very great, and the authorities to be consulted many; and perhaps the almost total absence—as in this case—of a documentary history of the building of the fabric, makes for a larger bulk of pamphlets and of communications to the antiquarian journals. Whether or no theory be wiser than fact, it is certainly more voluminous. Besides the books and papers mentioned in their place, I have especially to express my indebtedness to the work on Lichfield by the Rev. William Beresford, one of the "Diocesan Histories" Series, and to the "Handbook of Lichfield Cathedral" by the late John Hewitt, the well-known antiquarian. I have also to thank Mr R. R. Redmayne of Lichfield for much valuable information, as also Mr C. Harradine, the Principal Verger, whose interest in and knowledge of the Cathedral are well known in Lichfield; and the Photochrom Co. Ltd., Messrs S. B. Bolas & Co., and Mr F. G. M. Beaumont, for the excellent photographs they have allowed me to reproduce.

A. B. CLIFTON.

CONTENTS

PAGE

CHAPTER I.—History of the Cathedral 3

CHAPTER II.—Description of the Exterior 30
The Close 33
Bishop's Palace 34
Spires 35
West Front 39
North Doorway 48
Lady Chapel 50
South Transept 51
Bells 52

CHAPTER III.—Description of the Interior . . . 54
Nave 54
Pulpit, Lectern, etc. 64
North Aisle of Nave—Monuments and Glass . . 64
South Aisle of Nave—Monuments and Glass . . 67
Transepts 67
Organ 71
Choir 75
Screen and Stalls 84
Reredos 87
Sedilia and Pavements 88
Monuments and Glass in the Choir . . . 91
Lady Chapel 100
Sacristy and Chapel of St. Chad's Head . . . 106
Chapter-House 110
Library 113

CHAPTER IV.—History of the See 117

ILLUSTRATIONS

PAGE

Cathedral from the West . . . . . . *Frontispiece*
Arms of the See . . . . *Title page*
South Prospect of the Cathedral (Old Print) 2
Cathedral from Stowe Church (Old Print) 13
Ancient Gateway in the Close 17
South Transept in 1813—Exterior 23
Cathedral from the South 31
Cathedral from the Minster Pool 37
Great West Doorway in 1813 42
Great West Doorway 43
Southern Doorway in West Front 46
Bay of the Nave—Exterior 48
North Entrance in 1813 49
Bay of the Choir—Exterior 50
Doorway of South Transept 51
Bay of the Nave—Interior 55
Bay of the Choir—Interior 56
Nave in 1813—Interior 57
Nave, looking East 59
Nave, looking West 61
North Aisle of Nave, looking East 64
Arcade with Semi-Effigy 68
Detail of Semi-Effigy 69
Choir in 1820—Interior 77
Choir, looking East 79
South Choir Aisle 80
Choir, looking West 81
Under the Central Tower 85
Reredos 89
The Sleeping Children 95
Fresco in South Choir Aisle 97
Brackets in Lady Chapel 100, 104
Capital in Chapter-House 108
Chapter-House 109
Arcade in Chapter-House 111
The Gospels of St. Chad 115
Monument to Dr Johnson 136

PLAN OF THE CATHEDRAL 137

A

Hollands Garston arm: Fil: &
Hered: Dom: Johis Garston
de Mincshull in Com: Stafford
Bar.t Hæc Tabella dicata est.

The South Prospect of the Cathedral Church of St Mary & St Chad at Lichfield

LICHFIELD CATHEDRAL

CHAPTER I

THE HISTORY OF THE CATHEDRAL

THE cathedral of Lichfield, as we now know it, was built at various times in the thirteenth century and the early part of the fourteenth; and but for some comparatively slight and obvious alterations, it is therefore entirely in the styles known as Early English and Decorated. Unhappily nearly all the early archives and documents belonging to the cathedral are lost, having been destroyed in the time of the Civil Wars by the soldiery who sacked the place after the siege of the close by the forces of the Parliament. The absence of all documentary evidence as to the dates of the various parts of the cathedral has been much regretted by antiquarians, since it would be hard to find a better example of the gradual change which English church architecture was undergoing during the very busy period when this cathedral must have been built. Here we have the rigid simplicity of the Early English style in the transepts, giving place in the nave to the luxury of the Early Decorated, with its geometrical tracery; while in the Lady Chapel and presbytery we find an example, in some respects unique, of the gorgeousness of the completely evolved Decorated style. To know exactly when each part was built would be to add to our knowledge of architectural chronology; but instead, we must employ what knowledge we already possess, and by reasoning the very converse of what we could wish to have been able to use, we can arrive at an approximate history of the structure of the cathedral.

Not so long ago Oswy had the credit of having built the cathedral, and later it was set down to Roger de Clinton. Modern criticism as easily disposes of the claims of the latter

as of the former, and there can be no doubt that no part of
the present cathedral is of earlier date than 1200 A.D.

Much valuable information as to the cathedral, which
Clinton may have had a part in building, was obtained in
1860, when, for the alterations which were then in progress,
excavations were made in the choir. The result of his in-
vestigations Professor Willis published in an article in the
Archæological Journal for 1861, entitled "Memoir on the
Foundations of Early Buildings recently discovered at Lichfield
Cathedral," and the theory which he there set out as to the
history of the cathedral has been generally accepted by antiquarians. Nothing can be more interesting than this article,
but it is too full of detail for anything beyond the bare results
of Professor Willis's reasoning to be given here : these are
set out in their place.

Of the early Saxon church which was erected on this site
practically nothing is known, but it is supposed to have been
built by Bishop Hedda at the close of the seventh century,
and of stone taken from Roman ruins in the neighbourhood, though there is really no evidence to support this
theory. The desire to find another instance of the waste
material and sites once dedicated to a pagan religion being
used by the victorious Christian church may have something
to do with such a legend. Nothing except tradition is left of
this church, to which it is said the bones of St. Chad were
removed from Stowe. Probably in the four or five hundred
years which elapsed before the Norman cathedral was built,
several churches succeeded one another on or about the
present site : whatever happened, we know nothing.

Our real knowledge commences with the Norman cathedral.
The excavations already spoken of laid bare small portions of
its foundations, and from these Professor Willis decided that the
Norman choir had a semi-circular apse, and extended from the
central tower to about the middle of the fifth bay of the present
choir ; while the exterior line of its side walls nearly corre-
sponded with the interior line of the present aisle. The Norman
building probably possessed transepts, but these certainly had
no aisles ; the rest is conjecture, but from other Norman
cathedrals and churches which are in existence we can fairly
well imagine what it was like. The altar probably stood over
the centre of the semi-circle of the apse, while the bishop's

throne was behind it, facing west, with the canons' stalls spreading out down the choir, and the choir stalls continuing them right down under the tower into the nave : or perhaps there were no seats for the choir in those days—we do not know; but there must have been a processional path round the altar. We can imagine, too, the massive masonry of the pillars with their heavy capitals and circular arches. To think of a Norman church is to think possibly of Peterborough; and Lichfield Cathedral, no doubt, was like that minster, but on a very much smaller scale.

There is no record as to when the Norman church was built, but Robert de Lymesey, the bishop, is said in 1088 to have used a large quantity of silver, which he took from the church at Coventry, in extensive buildings in Lichfield; and Roger de Clinton is declared to have exalted the church as well in building as in honour, so he may have erected, or helped to erect, the Norman cathedral. Nothing whatever remains above ground of this building, which was probably taken down gradually while the cathedral which now stands in its place was being erected. Before this was done, however, there was added a rectangular chapel to the east of the Norman apsidal choir, which, with it, must have extended nearly to the end of the seventh bay of the present choir. Nothing is known of it beyond the fact that the foundations were discovered and examined by Professor Willis, who decided that it was probably built late in the twelfth century, and that its existence, if it was ever finished, must have been short.

Very early in the thirteenth century the first part of the present building was begun by erecting a rectangular choir just outside the walls of the Norman choir, which must have been then removed. This new Early English choir (including the presbytery) extended from the central tower to the end of the seventh bay of the present choir. It will be found that the eastern portion of this was subsequently removed, but the western half still remains, and can readily be distinguished from the Decorated part. The high altar of this period must have stood just to the west of the space between the fifth piers, thus leaving the space between the fifth and sixth piers as a processional path between the two side aisles; while against the eastern wall were four altars, one at the end of each aisle and two between them. At the same time that this choir was built, was also built on the south side the sacristy, with the room adjoining it : these both remain.

The next alteration took place about 1220, and was the erection of a new south transept in place of the Norman one, which, as has been said, almost certainly had no aisle ; then followed in about twenty years the north transept and the chapter-house, with its vestibule, all these buildings being in the Early English style, though the difference in their times of erection is clearly marked in their details. Two royal licences to dig Hopwas stone for " the new fabric of the church at Lichfield " in 1235 and 1238 are evidence that work was going on about this time ; and the desire of Henry III. (which is more fully set out in the description of the interior of the transept) to have a roof at Windsor like that of Lichfield gives an almost documental certainty to the architectural theory that the transepts were built at the time above stated.

No historical document exists that can apply to the building of the nave ; but that must have come next, and have been in progress almost before the north transept could have been finished. The west front was commenced somewhere about the beginning of the last quarter of the thirteenth century, and, including the two towers which form such an important part of it, must have taken a very long time to complete. From the thorough examination made when the recent restorations were in progress, it was decided that these towers were built in three distinct stages—the lowest, which just included the row of kings, being assigned to about 1280 ; the next stage to 1300 ; and the upper part, including the belfry windows, to about 1330, while the spires were not finished till some time after.

Walter de Langton became bishop in 1296, and of him it is distinctly recorded that he commenced the Lady Chapel. From an old register in the Salt Library at Stafford, it appears that Langton left £80, 13s. 3d. for the building of the chapel. He died in 1321. And, in 1323, there is another entry showing that the chapter came to some agreement with his executor by which each party should pay half the cost of finding a quarry for the stone ; so that it does not appear that building operations had proceeded very far at his death. It is interesting to note, as the same source shows us, that the money left by the bishop was partly on loan to King Edward II. for the expenses of his wars with Scotland, which wars had ended so disastrously at

Bannockburn. In the following reign, Edward III. was asked by the chapter to repay what was still owing of this money.

The Lady Chapel was probably erected beyond the eastern end of the church as it then stood; and while this was being done, the Early English presbytery was taken down and rebuilt in the Decorated style to match the new Lady Chapel, and the old clerestory of the choir was also rebuilt in the same style. The main idea was to obtain uniformity; but as it apparently was not proposed to take down the sacristy on the south, nor the chapter-house on the north, it was not considered necessary to pull down the choir—*i.e.* the last three western bays—any lower than the triforium; for the lower parts would be hidden by these buildings from the outside, and inside various shifts were resorted to to obtain uniformity. The work almost certainly grew from east to west gradually, as the clerestory of the choir end is lighter than that of the eastern or presbytery end; so that no doubt the pulling down of the old choir clerestory was only done after the building of the eastern end made it seem better to alter the rest into uniformity. With regard to the inside effect, Professor Willis says: "The front half of their pier arches (those belonging to the three western bays), however was removed and mouldings given them corresponding to those of the new presbytery. Their piers also were slightly altered, although partially concealed by the choir stalls. By these arrangements the aspect of the whole interior of the choir and presbytery was made uniform." How far this theory is sound will be seen when the alterations early in the present century are considered in their place.

Bishop Langton also erected the shrine of St. Chad at an expense of £2000. This shrine stood behind the high altar in the most eastern bay of the retro-choir, and, as was usual, had on its western side an altar dedicated to the saint. A similar arrangement can still be seen in Westminster Abbey, where the shrine of Edward the Confessor stands behind the reredos. The space behind the reredos, with the corresponding bays of the aisles, were in the past called the lady choir. This portion was separated from the rest of the choir by the reredos in the centre, and by screens in a line with the reredos in the aisles; there was a chapel in the lady choir at the end of each aisle, but to whom they were dedicated is doubtful. Stukeley, writing in 1715, says: "In St. Peter's Chapel, which is now a place to lay scaffolding and ladders, etc., was painted upon the wall St. Peter crucified with his head downwards, and two other apostles, etc. And in this place is the noted St. Chad's tomb, though defaced, removed from the lady choir to be put here since the Restoration." The same writer also tells us that: "Over across the middle of the said choir was a rood loft, finely carved and gilded, and St. Chad's shrine, but destroyed in time of war."

Professor Willis has pointed out the singular parallelism between the development of this cathedral and that of York. "The Norman Cathedral of York was built in 1080, and that of Lichfield at an uncertain date. Between 1154-1181, Archbishop Roger substituted for the original chancel at York a long, square-ended choir, with the aisle carried behind the end. At Lichfield, during the same period, the large chapel was built at the end of the Norman apse; and about the beginning of the thirteenth century the whole Norman eastern termination was, as at York, replaced by a long, square-ended choir with the low aisles behind. Next, at York the Norman transepts were rebuilt in Early English: the south transept, 1230-1241; followed by the north transept, 1241-1260. Also at Lichfield the Norman transepts were rebuilt in Early English, beginning with the south and ending with the north. The Early English work of this cathedral is shown by the licences to dig stone to have been in progress in 1235 and 1238. York nave and Lichfield were next rebuilt in Early Decorated—the first in 1291-1324. Lastly, at Lichfield, the elongation of the eastern part was begun at the extreme east, beyond the existing choir by the Lady Chapel, in late Decorated under Bishop Langton, 1296-1321, and followed by taking down the choir, and continuing the same work on its site westward. The works at York followed in the same order, but forty or fifty years later, by first erecting the presbytery outside the existing choir, and then taking down the latter and continuing the work of the presbytery to form the new choir. The plans of the two cathedrals rival each other in the simplicity of their proportions."

One other important thing which Bishop Langton did was to fortify, or at any rate to add greatly to the fortifications of the cathedral. He surrounded the close with a high stone wall and constructed "two beautiful gates" on the west and south sides of the close. Truly, had he been able to see the result of his fortification, he might have said with the Preacher: "All is vanity and vexation of spirit"; for if there was one thing which brought down on the cathedral the extremities of hatred and violence in the Civil Wars, it was that it proved able to be held as a fortress against those who came up against it.

Bishop Langton built also the palace, which for so long, with its towers and turrets, stood in the north-east corner of the close. It must have been a magnificent building, and we know that its hall was decorated with frescoes of scenes in the recent wars. It was destroyed after the siege of the close in 1643, and Fuller, writing about that time, speaks of it as the "invisible castle now vanished out of sight."

Roger de Norburg completed the Lady Chapel and the new presbytery, and was succeeded by Robert de Stretton, who (as we discover from a document dated 1390, four years after his death) completed St. Chad's shrine; for that is the only meaning which can be given to the wording of the bond, that the vicar's choral should offer prayers for, amongst others, "Robert Stretton, bishop, for making St. Chadd's shrine, and for giving them £24 to continue amongst them."

There has recently been discovered among the muniments of the chapter, an indenture dated in 1345 or 1346, and made between the sacrist on the one hand, and the dean and chapter on the other, for the safe custody of the goods in the sacristy. The "goods" are too numerous for a list of them to be given, but they include "the head of Blessed Chad, in a certain painted wooden case; also an arm of Blessed Chad; also bones of the said saint in a certain portable shrine." Then follows a list of the bones and relics of a large number of saints, including part of the sepulchre of Our Lord, and part of St. Peter's cross. There were also crosses, gold, and silver, and jewelled—a large number of many kinds, all set out separately—mitres, jewels, chalices, copes, and every kind of vestment of the most gorgeous description. Bishops and kings and queens had apparently showered their wealth and valuables upon the cathedral; and with the subscriptions of the diocese, known as Chad's Pennies, and the offerings of pilgrims, the riches of the cathedral seem to have been enormous. These "goods," in many cases with their donors' names, are all set out in the roll, which, it is interesting to notice, is dated in the year of the Black Death; possibly the enormous mortality of the time may have made it seem necessary that the mere memory of man should not be depended upon when so few seemed likely to survive. To read the list is to get some notion of the magnificence of the services; and it is no wonder that pilgrims came from all parts of the diocese, and of England, to worship where so many relics were collected. The mid-Sunday in Lent was originally the time, afterwards Whitsuntide, for the crowds to attend the cathedral. They were shown the head of St. Chad, probably from the little gallery in the south aisle of the choir, and then they laid their offerings at the great shrine, on which were lying the other relics of the saint.

No doubt the early part of the fifteenth century was the period when the cathedral was most glorious within and without. Fuller, in his "Church History," published in 1655, from which quotation has already been made, after giving an account of the building of the cathedral, says: "But now in the time of the aforesaid William Heyworth, the Cathedral of Litchfield was in the verticall height thereof, being (though not augmented in the essentials) beautified in the ornamentals thereof. Indeed, the West front thereof is a stately Fabrick, adorned with exquisite imagerie, which I suspect our age is so far from being able to imitate the workmanship that it understandeth not the Historie thereof. Surely what Charles the Fifth is said to have said of the citie of Florence, that it is a pittie it should be seen save only on Holy-dayes; as also that it was fit that so fair a Citie should have a Case and Cover for it to keep it from wind and weather, so in some sort, this Fabrick may seem to deserve a shelter to secure it. But alas! it is now in a pittiful case—indeed, almost beaten down to the ground in our civil dissensions. Now, lest the Church should follow the Castle — I mean quite vanish out of view — I have, at the cost of my worthy friend here exemplified the Portraiture thereof; and am glad to hear it to be the design of ingenious persons to preserve ancient churches in the like nature (whereof many are done in this, and more expected in the next part of Monasticon), seeing when their substance is gone, their verie shadows will be acceptable to posteritie."

In the fifteenth century a library was built outside the

door of the north transept, but a little to the west; it was quite separate from the cathedral. This was one of the gifts of Dean Heywood (1457-1493). It is recorded that he gave £40 towards the building of it, but died before it was completed, and this was done by his successor, Dean Yotton, who also contributed to its erection. According to the statement in "*Anglia Sacra*" it was finished in the year 1500. It is marked in the plan of Browne Willis, 1727, and was taken down about 1750.

Some time in this century saw a change in the tracery of many of the windows. It may be that the introduction of printing was responsible for this change, and that the greater amount of light admitted by the windows of the Perpendicular style made their insertion advisable; or it may be that the tracery of windows being naturally fragile, in many cases a renewal became necessary, and the new Gothic style was naturally considered the best. Whatever the reason, the new Perpendicular tracery was inserted in many of the windows just as it was in a large number of cathedrals and churches all over England.

In reading the history of the building of this fabric, we cannot help noticing that even the great Gothic builders could not leave well alone. Then, as now, Fashion was the ruling power. Having a Norman church, they altered it into an Early English one; then they pulled down a good deal of this to get a more Decorated building; and finally they changed the windows in order to give the whole a Perpendicular appearance: side by side with other reasons that actuated them, they did their best to keep their cathedral in the fashion.

In the sixteenth century, Henry VIII., the great destroyer of religious houses, made but little difference to the fabric of this cathedral, but he laid his hands on the valuables. The shrine of St. Chad was denuded of its jewels, and everything which could be turned into money was taken away: much of it was fortunately returned for the "necessary uses" of the cathedral, but the services and ritual must have been much impaired and their beauty diminished. During this century, however, the cathedral gradually recovered, and we know that early in the next the services were again very much on the same scale of magnificence as they had been when the good bishops Patteshull and Weseham directed the diocese.

The next event in the history of the building is one which is necessarily referred to many times in this book. The siege of Lichfield Cathedral is probably the most famous incident in its long career ; not only on account of the immense injury done to the fabric itself, to its monuments and its decorations, but also on account of the "miraculous intervention" on behalf of the holy building, an intervention which, viewed with nine-teenth-century scepticism, does not appear to have done the cathedral any obvious good, but which at the time appears to have been treated with all the deference due to a genuine miracle.

The great Civil War began on August 22, 1642, when Charles I. set up his standard at Nottingham. At Lichfield, as everywhere else in England, there were partisans of both sides. The cathedral group was naturally for the king, while others, for one reason or another, joined either the Royal Party or the Parliamentarian. After Edgehill, which was fought in the autumn, matters became more and more serious in the Midlands ; and finally, in February 1643, the Royalists at Lichfield, hearing that at any moment an outbreak might take place, garrisoned the close, which ever since the days of Walter de Langton had been strongly fortified. They hoisted the king's flag on the great steeple, and waited the result. They had not long to wait. With March Lord Brooke, one of the fiercest of anti-churchmen, arrived in command of a strong body of Roundheads, and on the 2nd the siege commenced.

Lord Brooke was a fanatic, and ever fierce against cathedrals, he had, according to the diary of Archbishop Laud, two years before, as he was passing in a boat upon the Thames, said he hoped to see St. Paul's with not one stone left upon another. It was in this spirit that he set about the siege of the cathedral, and of his fate there are many accounts. Perhaps the following, taken from Dugdale's "View of the Late Troubles in England," is as good as any :—"This lord (Lord Brooke) being strangely tainted with fanatic principles, by the influence of one of his near relations, and some schismatical preachers (though in his own nature a very civil and well-humoured man), became thereby so great a zealot

THE CATHEDRAL FROM STOWE CHURCH.

[From Shaw's "History and Antiquities of Staffordshire," 1798.

against the established discipline of the Church, that no less than the utter extirpation of Episcopacy, and abolishing all decent order in the service of God, would satisfy him; to which end he became leader of all the power he could raise for the destruction of the cathedral of that diocese of Coventry and Litchfield. In order whereunto, when he had marched within half a mile of Litchfield, he drew up his army, and then devoutly prayed a blessing upon his intended works; withal earnestly desiring that God would, by some special token, manifest upon them His approbation of that their design: which being done, he went on and planted his great guns against the south-east gate of the close, himself standing in a window of a little house near thereto, to direct the gunners in their supposed battery; but it so happened that, there being two persons placed in the battlement of the chiefest steeple to make shot with long fouling guns at the cannoniers, upon a sudden accident, which caused the soldiers to give a shout, this lord, coming to the door (completely harnessed with plate armour *cap-à-pie*) was suddenly shot into one of his eyes; but the strength of the bullet, so much abated by the glance thereof on a piece of timber which supported a pentiss over the door, that it only lodged in his brains, whereupon he suddenly fell down dead; nor is it less notable that this accident fell out on the second day of March, which is the festival of that sometime famous Bishop S. Chad, to whose memory Offa, King of the Mercians, first erected this stately church and devoutly dedicated it."

Tradition has always asserted that the shot which killed Lord Brooke was fired by one of the sons of Sir Richard Dyott, who, with the Earl of Chesterfield, was commanding the cathedral garrison. This son was deaf and dumb, and was known as "Dumb Dyott." The gun is preserved in the family, and they are supported by other historians, disagreeing with Dugdale, in their account that the shot was no accidental one, but that Dyott, who was an accomplished marksman, recognising Lord Brooke, aimed at him and killed him.

In those days—and indeed even to the present day—it was believed that one who was afflicted with dumbness, idiocy, or any natural disease which showed God's hand, was especially His agent. Dumb Dyott was looked upon as being the agent of divine vengeance, and the fact of its being St. Chad's

Day strengthened the belief.   Here is an extract from a very
courtly letter written a few days afterwards by a young cavalier
to Lady Dyer; in it the feeling that a miracle had been
performed is clearly shown.   The writer says: "We have
had the honour in these parts to bring my Lord Brooke to
a quiet condition.   That enemy of our Church (March 2) was
slain in his quarrel against our Church, by the God of our
Church, with a shot out of the Cathedral, by a bullet made
of Church lead, through the mouth which reviled our Church;
and (if this be worth your reading) this Cathedral was dedicated to the memory of an old Saxon holy man (called Ceadda,
commonly Chad); the blow of death came from St. Chad's
Church upon St. Chad's Day.   This, being a verity, is fit for
a lady of rare worth."   The incident is constantly referred
to in contemporary literature, where the miracles claimed on
behalf of the Royalist party are worthy of a better result.
One more quotation will suffice.   The celebrated preacher,
Dr South, in his sermon on the text, "God hath loved the
gates of Sion more than all the dwellings of Jacob," says:
"Nor is that instance to be passed over of a commander
in the Parliamentary army, who, coming to rifle and deface
the cathedral at Lichfield, solemnly, at the head of his troops,
begged God to show some remarkable token of His approbation or dislike of the work they were going about.   Immediately after which, he was shot in the forehead by a deaf
and dumb man; and this was on St. Chad's Day, the name
of which saint that church bare, being dedicated to God in
memory of the same: where we see that as he asked of God
a sign, so God gave him one in the forehead, and that with
such a mark as he is like to be known by all posterity."

The house in which Lord Brooke was killed is in Dam
Street, at a distance, it is said, of about 185 yards from the
central spire of the cathedral; the late Mr Green caused the
following inscription to be put up over the doorway:—

"*March* 2, 1643.—Lord Brooke, a general of the Parliament forces preparing to besiege the Close of Lichfield, then
garrisoned for King Charles the First, received his death
wound on the spot beneath this inscription by a shot in the
forehead from Mr Dyott, a gentleman who had placed himself
on the battlements of the great steeple to annoy the besiegers."

The death of Lord Brooke was kept a secret as much as

possible, for fear the soldiers should indeed take it for a sign ; Sir John Gell was appointed in his place, and the siege continued. Under his direction "all such townsmen that had any sons, apprentises, or other servants within the close, and likewise all citizens' wives that had their husbands there, whether magistrates or other persons whatsoever," were collected together and put in the front of the soldiers against the close, but after a while, it not appearing to make much difference, they were all sent home again. The close meanwhile had been bombarded with cannon, and finally there arrived from Coventry a new engine, called a mortar, which cast burning shells. Most of these fell into the mill pool or went over the close altogether ; but it is said to have caused so much fright, no one there having seen such an engine before, that the Earl of Chesterfield, knowing also that his provisions could not last another day, and that there was little likelihood of their being reinforced, decided to yield the close on the best terms he could. These included free quarter to all, and on the 5th March, after a siege of three days, the close was yielded.

The damage that had been done was terrible ; not only was the whole fabric much injured, and all the stained glass destroyed, but the great steeple had been blown down and had in its fall broken in the roof of the church in several places. But even now the work of desecration was not complete. The close having been taken, the Parliamentary forces and their prisoners were all housed in and round the cathedral, and the most sacrilegious conduct is attributed to the former. The wanton soldiers pulled down the curious carved work, and battered in pieces what was left of the beautiful old stained glass ; they stripped the gravestones of their brasses, and destroyed the ancient records which were stored in the cathedral. These acts of destruction were no doubt due to the religious mania of the Roundheads against any form of ceremony or beauty in the House or Service of God ; but their passion became keener when they found what rich spoils were ready to their hands. It happened during their riotous proceedings that one of the soldiers raised the covering of the tomb containing the remains of Bishop Scrope, and found in it a silver chalice and a crozier of considerable value. This discovery naturally excited the soldiers, and every

ANCIENT GATEWAY FORMERLY IN THE CLOSE.

[From a Print dated 1773.

B

tomb was at once taken to pieces and its contents scattered; it is not wonderful therefore that the tombs that remain to the present day are few in number and these terribly mutilated. The crozier was afterwards sold to Elias Ashmole, the antiquarian, who took so great an interest in Lichfield. Nor was the sacrilege confined to destruction and spoliation. Dugdale tells us that "every day they hunted a cat with hounds through the church, delighting themselves with the echo from the goodly vaulted roof; and to add to their wickedness, brought a calf into it, wrapt in linen; carried it to the font, sprinkled it with water; and gave it a name in scorn and derision of that holy sacrament of baptism."

Not for long, however, did the Roundheads remain in possession. Prince Rupert was sent from Oxford, the head-quarters of the Royalist party at the time, to retake Lichfield. Having taken Bromicham on the way, he arrived at Lichfield with a strong force, and history repeated itself. The town offered no opposition, and Rupert had to lay siege to the close, which now was better garrisoned. The Royalists erected batteries on the north side, and kept up a heavy fire; they also attempted to undermine the walls, and finally succeeded in blowing up one of the towers of the close, and a fierce encounter took place, in which many men were slaughtered on both sides. At length, after ten days' siege, the close was surrendered to the king by the governor, who probably got better terms than he expected, as Rupert was required at Reading. The articles of capitulation are referred to by Clarendon as being most honourable, and are as follow :—

"It is consented by Colonel Hastings, by the authority given him by his highness Prince Rupert, that, in consideration of the delivery and yielding up of the Close of Lichfield, Lieutenant-Colonel Russel, and all the Captains and Officers with him, shall march out of the said Close, to-morrow being the one and twentieth day of this instant April, by ten o'clock in the morning, with fourscore men and musquetts, with flying colours, and fourscore horsemen, with arms belonging to them, and all other persons within the said Close to be at liberty to goe whither they please; and for their better and safe conveyance, a free pass or convoy from his highnesse, and eleven carts to convey away such goods as belong to any of the officers or soldiers, with themselves, to the City of

Coventry ; and that all prisoners shall be released on both sides, which have been taken in the City of Stafford since the coming down of the Right Honourable Lord Brooke. In witness whereof, we have hereunto put our hand and seal, this twentieth day of April A.D. 1643.   H. HASTINGS."

Russel did not leave empty-handed, as he is said to have taken away the communion plate and linen, and whatever else was of value. He was succeeded in command of the close by Colonel Bagot, who held it until 1646, when in the general ruin of the king's affairs the close was again taken.

In " *Mercurius Aulicus* " there is an interesting anecdote which shows the state of feeling between the two parties. A certain Captain Hunt, who had a command in the neighbouring town of Tamworth, sent Colonel Bagot the following challenge :—" Bagot, thou sonne of an Egyptian . . . meete mee half the way to-morrow morning, the half-way betwixt Tamworth and Litchfeald, if thou darest ; if not, I will whippe whensoever I meete thee. Tamworth, this December 1644. —THOMAS HUNT." Colonel Bagot did not neglect the challenge, and though he did not succeed in taking him prisoner, he "whipped " him home to Tamworth.

During the time Colonel Bagot was governor the post can have been no sinecure, for although there was no regular siege to be compared to the two just described, yet, lying as it did with so many Parliamentary strongholds in the immediate neighbourhood, this period cannot have been one of peace ; and Dr Harwood, in his " History of Lichfield," goes so far as to say that the close was frequently in a state of seige at this period. The battle of Naseby was fought on the 14th June 1645, with disastrous effect to the king. Colonel Bagot was present with 200 men, and no doubt escorted the king back to Lichfield, for he lay there for at least one night, and received an address from his faithful citizens, which, from its wording, shows that there was little hope left in his side. The king came again later in the year, and about March in the following year, 1646, the last siege commenced. It was a desultory affair compared to the first two, and only ended when the Royalists, in July, finding that the king had practically no real army in the field anywhere, surrendered again on terms which were most honourable to both sides.

The damage done to the cathedral in these times was esti-

mated at £14,000, which was for these days a very large
amount.   Some of the losses are thus particularised :

For a pair of organs broke in pieces,	.	£200
The destruction of the vicars' seats,	. .	600
The defacing of Lord Paget's tomb, which was executed in Italy,	. . . .	700

But enough has been said to show that the cathedral was in
a most ruinous state, and so it remained until a twelvemonth
after the Restoration.   From a manuscript in the Ashmolean
Collection at Oxford, it appears that Elias Ashmole had an
interview with the king in June 1660 as to the condition of the
cathedral.   The memorandum reads : " 16 June 1660.   This
morning Mr Rawlins of Lichfield tould me that the Clearke
Viccars of the Cathedrall Church had entered the Chapter-
house and there said service ; and this when the Vestry was
the only place in the Church yt had a roof to shelter them.
This very afternoon, I, having an opportunity to waite on the
Kg, and being in his Closet, tould him that the aforesaid
remaining number of poore Clearks Vicarrs had assembled in
the aforesaid place, and there kept their Canonicall houres and
prayd for his Maty, which he was pleased to heare.   Upon
further discourse, I acquainted him with the desolacion of the
place, wch he much lamented, and said he had been informed
that Winchestre Cathedrall had exceedingly suffred in these
late tymes, and that they had turnd it into Brewhouses, Malt-
houses, etc."   And again, on " July 18, 1660, Mr Dugdale
moved Dr Sheldon to become an instrument for the repair of
Lichfield Cathedral ; and proposed that the prebends, etc., that
were admitted should part with one-half of their profits towards
the repair of the fabrick, which would be no great burden to
them ; and by this example the gentry would be invited to join
with them in some considerable contribution.   N.B.—I find
this method succeeded accordingly."

The see was vacant for nearly a year after the Restoration, as
Bishop Frewen, who had been appointed to the see by Charles
I., was almost at once made Archbishop of York.   At last, in
December 1661, John Hacket, Doctor of Divinity of Trinity
College, Cambridge, was appointed, and he at once set himself
to the repair of the dilapidated cathedral ; on the very morn-
ing of his arrival at Lichfield he is said to have set his carriage-

horses and servants to the work of clearing out the rubbish, and with his own hands to have set them an example at the start. The work to be done must have appeared to be almost impossible of completion, for the central spire was still lying in ruins over the chapter-house and choir, the roof was broken in, and the pavements completely destroyed : everything was ruinous, for the Parliamentary folk had during the Common-wealth seized all materials which seemed to be of use for the repair of the dwelling-houses in the close and neighbourhood. However, the work progressed ; the bishop was so energetic that he was able to collect in the surrounding country about £8000, and so generous that he subscribed himself a sum of £1683, 12s. : and in eight years he succeeded in restoring the beauty of the cathedral.

The service at which it was re-consecrated was of great solemnity and ceremony : " His lordship, being arrayed in his episcopal vestments, attended by the dean, dignitaries, pre-bendaries, and other members of the Church, accompanied by many of the nobility and gentry, the bailiffs, citizens, and other public officers of the city and county of Lichfield, with an immense concourse of people, entered at the great west doors of the Cathedral. The vicars, choristers, etc., first walked up the south aisle of the Church, where the bishop with a loud voice repeated the first verse of the 144th psalm. Afterwards the whole choir alternately sang the psalm to the organ. In the same order they proceeded to the north aisle. The bishop sang the 100th psalm, which was repeated by the whole company. Then the train passed to the body of the Church, where the bishop began the 102nd psalm, which when the vicars choral had concluded, he commanded the doors of the choir to be opened, and in the same form, first encompassed the south side. The bishop began the first verse of the 122nd psalm ; the company finished it, and with the like ceremony proceeded to the north side, and sang the 131st psalm." The procession over, the bishop knelt down in the centre of the choir and prayed silently ; and then with a loud voice called on all the people to join with him in the Lord's Prayer, which was followed by other prayers suitable to the occasion. He then pronounced a solemn benediction on the act in which they were engaged, and upon all that were present. The usual service of morning prayer followed, with

two special anthems, and a collection—not for the cathedral—
but for the poor of the parish. The bishop also gave three
magnificent banquets—to the cathedral clergy, to the nobility of
the neighbourhood, and to the principal citizens of the city.

Thus concluded the ceremony of re-consecration, a work
which left the cathedral, not, unhappily, as it was when the first
siege took place, but still a very beautiful edifice, with more of
the Perpendicular style about the windows than previously, and
with grievous signs here and there of the terrible misfortunes
it had weathered. Sir Christopher Wren is said to have
designed the new central spire, and to have acted as architect
to the re-builders ; but this is almost certainly not the case : his
advice may have been asked, but probably at the most he gave
it with regard to rich altar-piece in the Corinthian style which
was erected in front of the old screen behind the high altar.
At any rate, his signature appears on one of the sixteen papers
on this matter still preserved among the muniments of the
cathedral.

The king gave 200 fair timber trees out of Needwood forest,
and his brother, the Duke of York, afterwards King James II.,
gave the money for the tracery of the great west window.
This window remained until the recent alterations, when it was
replaced by one more in accordance with the original thirteenth
century style. The Duke of York's window, with its ill-
proportioned geometrical tracery, need not be regretted any
more than the removal of the heroic statue of his Majesty
King Charles II., which occupied the central niche above it.
The statue was principally remarkable for its ugliness, and for
the history of the stonemason who hewed it ; he afterwards
married a rich wife, and finally arrived at the dignity of
knighthood. Bishop Hacket adorned the church with new
stalls and with an organ which cost £600 ; and he also made
arrangements for new bells worthy of the cathedral. He
ordered six, and three of them were delivered in his life-time.
Only one—the tenor bell—however, was hung in time for the
good bishop to hear it. His biographer, Dr Plume, says :
" The first time it was rung, the bishop was very weak ; yet he
went out of his bed-chamber into the next room to hear it :
he seemed well pleased with the sound, and blessed God, who
had favoured him with life to hear it ; but at the same time
observed that it would be his passing-bell, and retiring into his

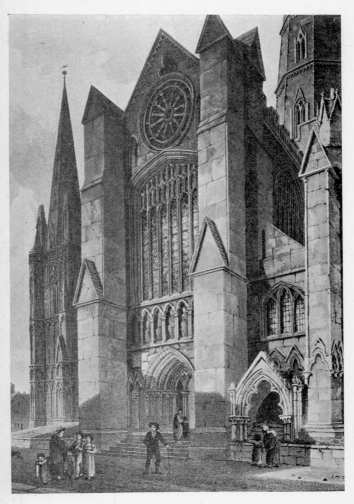

THE SOUTH TRANSEPT IN 1813

chamber, he never left it till he was carried to his grave." He
died in October 1670.

For some time the cathedral has no history to be recounted.
In 1750 we know that the ancient library outside the north
aisle, built by Deans Heywood and Yotton, was removed, and
the churchyard levelled ; we also know that the roof became
very defective, and the rain came in, so that a new roofing was
required.   Pennant tells us that the dean and chapter were
obliged to substitute slates instead of metal, on account of the
narrow revenues left to maintain this venerable pile ; and after
the strictest economy, they were under the necessity of con-
tributing from their own income in order to complete their
plan.

A few years later it was found that the fabric itself was in so
dilapidated a condition that much more extensive repairs were
necessary, and so Mr Wyatt, the celebrated architect, as Britton
calls him, came to Lichfield and began that scheme of alteration which has been the object of so much ridicule and con-
tempt.   To lovers of church architecture at the end of the
nineteenth century it seems astounding that the splendid and
inimitable cathedrals and churches of this country should have
been handed over every one to be destroyed and debased in the
way Wyatt destroyed and debased them.   But there is no doubt
that Wyatt represented the spirit of the time, just as Sir Gilbert
Scott represented the spirit of the middle of this century.
Then it was a love of " vistas " which actuated the alterations,
and caused the destruction of anything which came in the way
of what was considered a fine view.   In those days " vistas "
were the all-absorbing consideration and the subject of discussion amongst those who considered themselves cultured, as
may be seen in the novels of Jane Austen, and in " Mansfield
Park " in particular.   Later, the passion for replacing what was
old or worn by time with something new, something which
was supposed to be a reproduction of the old, has caused end-
less destruction.   The later passion has not yet disappeared,
unhappily ; but thankfully we may note the signs of the times,
and feel sure that in a few years neither a Wyatt with his
vistas and Roman cement, nor a Sir Gilbert with his cheap
statuettes and Italian trumperies, will be permitted under any
circumstances to lay a finger on what it has here and there
graciously pleased their forerunners to leave unspoiled.   How

little this is, can be judged by a visit to any cathedral church from Westminster Abbey downwards.

The achievements of Wyatt are recounted by Britton, who does not appear to have entirely decided whether he approved or not. Some of them, no doubt, were necessary; and it would be unfair to indiscriminately blame any architect who had to deal, however violently, with a building which had deteriorated, not merely in the pass of time, but also by the shock of war. Also a great deal of what Wyatt did was done for the sake of warmth, though the object in view, it is said, was not attained. Britton says that not only was there a general restoration of doors, windows, and flooring throughout, but also "two of the spires were partly rebuilt, the ends of the transepts were strengthened by new buttresses, the external roofs of the aisles were raised, and five divisions of the stone roof in the nave were taken down and replaced with plaster. The Lady Chapel was united with the choir by removing the screen which had been erected by Bishop Hacket. On taking this away, the workmen discovered the beautiful old screen which formed in all probability the original partition when the Lady Chapel was completed by the executors of Walter de Langton. This elaborate piece of architecture was in a very mutilated state; but Mr Wyatt, having restored it by the assistance of Roman cement to a very perfect condition, appropriated part of it to the new altar-piece, and the remainder to the organ screen or partition which divides the nave from the Choir," and which took up the whole of the western bay of the choir.

Since Britton's time it has been thought necessary to take another tone and to try to justify these alterations. Mr James Potter, the son of Mr Wyatt's chief assistant, who was afterwards architect to the cathedral, has endeavoured to prove that some of the alterations were unavoidable, and that the others were not made under Wyatt's advice, but in spite of it. Incidentally, in the course of a letter to the *Staffordshire Advertiser*, he speaks of the "unsightly and incongruous work of Wren's," in referring to the wooden reredos, and states that Wren had previously closed the arches of the four most western bays of the choir in order to receive the stalls. He also says : "But so completely did Wren perform his work of blocking-up that he took care to conceal every vestige of

moulding, both of the piers and the archivolts, leaving only
in view the clustered shafts from which the vaulting of the
roof sprang.   I have before noticed that Mr James Wyatt's
death occurred in A.D. 1813, and that this western portion of
the choir remained in the state in which Sir Christopher Wren
left it up to the following year.   In the early part of that year
the architect to the fabric, the late Mr Potter, was instructed
by the dean and chapter to cause the entire removal of the
old stall work and unmask the three arches (then concealed),
this being the space on either side of the choir occupied by
the stalls in question.   The arches being much dilapidated
and past restoration, Dean Woodhouse decided to have them
made to correspond with the decorated bays in an easterly
direction.   This work was executed, as also the canopy of
the new stalls, in Roman cement.   I cannot myself think
that Dean Woodhouse exhibited any degree of bad taste in
adopting the existing decorated arches as his model for the
new ones ; and, as regards the canopies of the new stalls, they
were exact resemblances of the old reredos, and surely no
modern architect will presume to find fault with them.   I
must here observe that the choice of material was not confined to the architect employed to carry out the work, but
was chosen by the dean and chapter, the state of the fabric
fund, out of which the whole of the expenses were defrayed, being insufficient to meet the outlay of a more costly
material."

The above account is most interesting, and, assuming that
the writer was correct in the facts as to what was done by
Wyatt and by his father, we are confronted with a difficulty.
From Professor Willis's account, already quoted, it is obvious
that he was of opinion that the alteration in the style of the
front of these pier arches was made in Gothic times.   Mr
Potter says it was done in the nineteenth century.   It is, of
course, possible for some alteration to have been made at
both these times ; but it looks as if the harmony was not
complete until recently, probably because the height of the
old stalls prevented the variations from being easily seen.   As
to Wren, Mr Potter probably was only repeating the recognised tradition that Wren was responsible for the rebuilding
by Bishop Hacket, and no argument can be deduced on this
point, the latest and best opinion being that there is, as already

stated, no evidence to prove that the great Sir Christopher had much to do with the cathedral.

Soon after Wyatt's death the policy of Roman cement, which he had inaugurated, was continued, and the whole of the west front become one mass of stucco and paste. The row of kings was replaced in this way, as also the statues in the great porch, and all the mouldings and decorations were covered with cement, and practically the whole cathedral from end to end had its deficiencies added to in this way. This work was completed about 1822. From then to 1856 the cathedral did not receive much alteration; but in the latter year Sir Gilbert, then Mr, Scott was called in, and the extensive alterations were commenced, which may be said scarcely to have finished in this year of 1897. It is not necessary to discuss here this restoration. It is sufficient to say that it has been the aim of those in authority to restore the cathedral to the appearance and arrangement it presented at the beginning of the seventeenth century. Wyatt's altera- tions received scant courtesy, and the cathedral as we now see it may be declared to be a triumph for the restorer—so great a triumph, indeed, that in many parts the unsuspicious admirer might be led to conclude that he was looking at a brand new edifice. Still, the cathedral has some of its old work left, and perhaps in the nave we are confronted with more of the work of the original Gothic builders than in any other part. What has been done in the last forty years is specifically discussed in the description of the exterior and interior in the two next chapters; but here it will be well to show what the condition of the cathedral was in the middle of the century, just before the recent restoration. Canon Lonsdale has given us a splendid description in his "Recollections," and if any- thing can reconcile us to the wholesale renewal which then took place, it will be found in the account which he gives in this little pamphlet, from which are now quoted the follow- ing sentences. He says: "The Nave and Transepts were absolutely empty of furniture of any kind, except that the South Transept contained the fittings of the Dean's Consistory Court (since abolished), and in the North Transept, on the spot where the organ now is, stood the statue of Bishop Ryder, raised on a high pedestal, and looking as if it were about to tumble forward. The walls, arches, and pillars were one uniform, dead, yellowish whitewash, many coats thick ; as also the Choir from end to end, and from top to bottom, and indeed the whole of the interior. . . . The Nave was quite unused ; indeed, except during service hours, the Verger's Silver Key alone gave admission to any part of the church. . . . The two parts of the building were altogether separate from each other.   The Choir was entered by a door under a high partition, composed of remains of the original High Altar, fourteenth century screen, and of other materials.   This partition filled the whole of the first bay of the present Choir.   On each side of the entrance were Vestries for the Lay Vicars and the Choristers, and above these was placed the organ; the rest of the space up to the Roof being filled in with glass, so that the separation of Nave and Choir was complete. . . . In the Choir itself the remains of the Reredos, which stood at the spot where the present one is now fixed, had been removed by Wyatt at the end of the last century, and the Holy Table was carried to the extreme East of the Lady Chapel.   On either side, from the screen up to the very entrance of the Lady Chapel, were pews made of oak lined with green baize and studded with brass nails.   The Choir Aisles on either side were entirely shut out from the Choir, the arches being filled in by plaster, in order, as was imagined, to help towards warmth. In the three bays eastward from the screen—the second, third, and fourth, as they are now—stalls were fixed, composed of plaster, wood, rope, nails, and much else, with canopies of the same material over them, which the old Verger of that day used to call 'beautiful Tabernacle work.'   The Dean and Canons' Residentiary had stalls facing eastward in the screen under the organ. . . . The Choir Aisles, shut out from the Choir, were long, narrow passages, never used, ending on the North side in a blank wall, and on the South with the monument of the 'Sleeping Children.' "

This was the inside of the Cathedral : the outside was stucco.   Such facts as these will have to be borne in mind when the next century passes judgment on Sir Gilbert Scott.   For us, it should be sufficient that we have judged Wyatt.

CHAPTER II

OF all the cathedral churches of England, Lichfield may be said to be the most lovely. Other cathedrals are larger—indeed, this is the smallest of them all—grander, or more magnificent; but for simple beauty, for charm, for delicacy of construction and appearance, Lichfield may rightly claim to take the foremost place. Peterborough, when we stand inside the west door and look down its line of enormous columns, fills us with awe at its immensity and strength : a feeling which is perhaps a little impaired by the present position of its stalls. Salisbury appeals to us with its perfect simplicity and symmetry, and York with its unequalled grandeur and splendour ; but after viewing all the cathedrals of England, it is Lichfield which is most likely to be remembered among them for something which may be most aptly called charm. What can be more delightful than the view which confronts the traveller who, approaching from the town, pauses to look across the sparkling water of the pool at the three graceful spires standing out amid a wealth of green trees and shrubs. Truly a picture to be long remembered. Here is, indeed, the precious jewel set in a silver sea.

The cathedral does not stand on high enough ground for any very fine view of the entire building to be obtained. But from whatever point in the neighbourhood of Lichfield we look we can see its three slender spires, grouping themselves, sometimes so that only two can be distinguished, sometimes so that they all appear in one cluster as though rising from one tower, and sometimes spreading out so that two seem to have very little connection with the third. For years they have been known as the "Ladies of the Vale"; they have looked down on many changes, and indeed have suffered changes themselves. They now rise from an almost new building—

30

THE CATHEDRAL FROM THE SOUTH.

new at anyrate in appearance. As we approach the cathedral either from Bird Street and face the west front, or from Dam Street and confront the south side of the Lady Chapel, the same sad feeling comes over us that all here is new. Even as these words are written the south side of the choir is being renovated, and no doubt what little of the old is still left will soon disappear. The west front, with its niches and images, is all new ; the south side of the nave is new, and indeed everywhere it is its newness that first strikes one. One cannot help wondering if this extreme severity of restoration is absolutely essential ; for if not essential, the vague disappointment might well turn to anger that in days when the art of architecture has become almost contemptible, it should be thought necessary to carry through such wholesale renewal of work, never to be replaced, belonging to the grand days of Gothic building. For this old work can never be replaced : it is a sad thought that in every art, the early groping days, when the new medium or the new method is hardly settled, and its limitations but imperfectly understood, produce the great work. It is so in literature, in music, in painting, in sculpture, and in architecture ; but it is only to the last that we dare to offer the assistance of our own less artistic age. The cathedral as we see it to-day has met with many vicissitudes. Of its misfortunes in the Civil Wars much has already been said ; and something of its sufferings at the hands of restorers. At present, after studying the west front and contemplating the extreme newness of its every detail, we can only hope that when age has somewhat staled the infinite variety of its modern ornament, future pilgrims to the shrine of St. Chad will not think too unkindly of an age given over to the rigours of restoration.

The Close.—The cathedral stands in a close which was once surrounded by strong walls with bastions and a moat. Nature had supplied the moat on the south side, and the Cathedral Pool, as it is now called, is still there. The artificial moat has been drained, but its course can be easily traced running round the bishop's palace, and its water has been replaced by lovely gardens and gravel walks. Some bits of the old walls remain, the north-east bastion in the palace gardens and a turret on a house at the south corner : the "beautiful gates" of Bishop Langton are gone ; but in the Vicars' Close at the west of the cathedral are two small irregular courtyards with houses so old that we feel sure that their wooden beams and plaster were there when the Royalists of the neighbourhood housed themselves within the fortified close.

The close is not large, and of course, as Lichfield is a cathedral of the old establishment, there are no monastical buildings, no ruined cloisters. On the north side the ground rises rapidly in a grassy slope to a terrace, behind which are some of the canons' houses. Opposite the north transept is the deanery, a substantial red brick house in the style of the middle of the last century ; next to it, and farther east, is the bishop's palace.

The Bishop's Palace is of stone, and was built by Thomas Wood, the bishop who succeeded Hacket, and who is said to have been compelled to erect it as a fine for his neglect of the diocese. It bears on the front the date 1687. The old palace of Bishop Langton, which occupied the same position in the close, was swept away in the Civil Wars. The bishops of Lichfield had another palace at Eccleshall until the time of Bishop Selwyn, who sold it, and with a portion of the money erected here the two unsightly wings and the still more unsightly chapel. In the palace gardens, in the south-west corner, stood the old bell-tower of the cathedral, of whose destruction in 1315 we have a record. From the bishop's garden there is a charming view through the trees of Stowe pool and St. Chad's Church apparently standing at its farther edge : its old towers stand out finely, and the gravestones in the churchyard remind us that in far-off Mercian days St. Chad was laid to rest in this very spot.

On the east side of the close is an unsightly white house which rises a blot on the otherwise beautiful view of the cathedral from Stowe ; next to it is a charming old building with the turret already mentioned.

On the south side is the entrance from Dam Street, with an old house at the corner. On this side also is the Theological College, a low ordinary-looking building, said to have been originally training-stables for race horses ; and farther west are more houses of the cathedral clergy. And behind all these is the pool. One cannot help agreeing with Britton in thinking what a delightful thing it would be for the close if all the houses on this side could be pulled down so that the cathedral might have nothing but grass and trees between it and the pool. Britton gives an imaginary view of the south side with all the houses cleared away.

On the west side of the cathedral is another entrance to the close, which runs between the Vicars' Close already mentioned and the hideous college built by Andrew Newton for the widows and orphans of clergymen.

The Cathedral is built of new red sandstone from quarries in the immediate neighbourhood of Lichfield itself. On Borrowcop, to the north (where tradition says two Mercian kings were killed, to be afterwards buried in the close), is the hole left by the cathedral; and on the other side, at Wheel Lane, is a quarry from which much stone, both red and white, has been taken for the recent repairs to the fabric. Its ruddy colour adds much to the picturesqueness of the building.

Mrs Van Rensselaer, in her interesting account of the English cathedrals, says : " In any and every aspect, but more especially when foliage comes close about it, Lichfield's colour assists its other beauties. Grey is the rule in English churches —dark cold grey at Ely, for example ; light yellow grey at Canterbury, and pale pearly grey at Salisbury ; and although dark greyness means great solemnity and grandeur, and light greyness great delicacy and charm, they both need the hand of time—the stain of the weather and the web of the lichen— to give them warmth and tone ; and the work of the hand of time has almost everywhere in England been effaced by the hand of the restorer. Red stone is warm and mellow in itself, and Lichfield is red with a beautiful soft ruddiness that could hardly be over-matched by the sandstone of any land."

The plan of the cathedral shows a simple cross, with a chapter-house (joined by a vestibule to the choir) on the north side, and a sacristy on the south side. It may also be noticed that the nave and the choir (including the presbytery) have each eight bays or severies, and that if we regard the bay under the central tower as a double one, the two transepts together have eight bays. Thus the transverse arm of the cross is of the same length as both the eastern arm and the western arm. There is a Lady Chapel at the eastern end of the choir, and there are aisles on each side of the nave and choir and on the eastern side of the transepts.

We have already seen that the cathedral has three **Spires**, and this is perhaps its most notable characteristic, for Lichfield is the only church now existing in England with this distinction. The cathedral at Coventry, so long the sister church of the diocese, and so ruthlessly destroyed by Henry VIII., had also three spires; as had Ripon Minster, but these were of lead, and have since been pulled down.

Of the spires, one rises from the central tower and one surmounts each of the towers which flank the west front. The central spire dates only from the Restoration, the older spire having been entirely destroyed in the Civil Wars. There is no doubt that the original spire was different in appearance to the present one, which is an imitation of the western spires, carried out in the spirit of the Perpendicular style. What the earlier spire was really like is doubtful, neither is it quite certain when it was built, though the central tower was probably rebuilt about 1250, when it is supposed that the intention was to retain the Norman nave. What the height and pitch of the roof of the old Norman nave must have been can be seen from the old housing course which remains to this day above the nave groining. "It was the custom," as Mr J. O. Scott explained in a lecture on the cathedral, "of old builders, as of modern builders, to insert in any wall against which a roof abuts a projecting course of stone, called a 'housing,' following the slope of the roof, the object being to keep the wet from getting in between the roof and the wall. And so when the central tower was rebuilt, there was the Norman nave to which the new work had to be fitted. Hence, at this time the builders inserted a 'housing course' of masonry into the west wall of the new tower, to protect the junction of the old Norman nave roof from the weather." These disused housing courses can constantly be seen in old churches, sometimes several, one above the other, showing the changes in the roofing of the church. The present spire is said vaguely to have been erected from the designs or under the direction of Sir Christopher Wren ; but the tradition which connects this great modern architect with the cathedral is probably untrustworthy.

The two western spires were probably built in Bishop Norburgh's time, and possibly were finished in the time of his successor; but the north-west spire has been rebuilt from the belfry windows upwards in imitation of the old work, but, like the central tower, in the Perpendicular manner. The south-

Photochrom Co. Ltd., Photo.]
THE CATHEDRAL FROM THE MINSTER POOL.

west or Jesus Tower, which is a little higher than the other, has also had its two upper storeys rebuilt. The spires are octagonal, and are divided into six compartments. In the western spires the four lower compartments have windows of two lights each with acute crocketted pediments. There are only four windows in the lowest compartment; but in the second, third, and fourth compartments there is a window in each face; the fifth is panelled between crocketted ribs, and the top compartment is plain with small windows. All the spires are open all the way up without any inside supports.

The central spire has the same number of compartments, with windows in all of them except the top; but there are only four windows in each compartment, facing north, east, west, and south. The top of the central spire is about 252 feet from the floor, and of the western spire about 193.

But if Lichfield's three spires are unique, so also is Lichfield's **West Front.** It is not, of course, very large, and it is not indeed as large as it might have been had the same means been employed here as were employed at Wells, where an exaggerated idea of size is attained by placing the towers outside the lines of the nave aisles. Here the two towers, which form so important a part of the front, are in their lowest stage merely part of the aisles, so that the whole width of the west front is very little greater than the width of the nave itself. The west front of Lichfield is noted for the richness of its decorations, covered as it is with niches holding images and, it might almost be said, with every available inch covered with decorative work. The whole has a most superb effect, and at a distance, where the poverty of the modern workmanship is not easily discerned, its appearance cannot be very different now to that which it presented at the end of the fourteenth century. Once again the niches are filled with statuary; but this work is nearly all new, and it is by some considered doubtful if any of the original remained in this century. It is, however, generally supposed, and not without good reason, that the five old statues which form part of the highest row in the north-west tower may have been original, and have escaped the general destruction which followed the Puritan capture of the cathedral. Three of the old statues are represented in the picture of the west front in Britton's "Cathedral Antiquities"; and in the interesting picture in

Fuller's "Church History," published in 1655, the west front is shewn with every niche filled; but there can be no doubt that this picture must have been made before the siege, or else it must have been drawn with the aid of memory from what remained afterwards.

This west front is flat, with octagonal turrets at each side, and consists of two towers and a central part. The central part has a doorway, a large window, and an acute pediment, the top point of the pediment being almost on a level with the parapet of the towers where the spires commence. These rise from between square pinnacles, enriched with feathered panels and crockets at the angles of the towers. The front is in three stages; the lowest stage contains the three doorways, and is surmounted by a very elaborate arcading filled with statues of kings. The second is covered with two storeys of arcading, and is divided into two parts by the large west window, above which is the pediment. The third stage consists of the upper part of the two towers; these are surmounted with parapets with lozenge-shaped mouldings inclosing quatrefoil and trefoil panels. There are windows to the belfry floors in this stage. Altogether, including these two belfry windows, there are only three windows in this front; this is unusual, as there are commonly windows at the west end of the nave aisles.

It is not easy to give a clear description of this front, or any which will convey its superb effect. As we see by the frontispiece, it is not only thickly covered with arcading and statues, but also it is very much enriched with trefoils, quatrefoils, and cinquefoils, especially in the spaces over the doors in the lowest stage, and in the pediment above the great window. The prevalence of the ball-flower decoration should not escape notice; upon the third stage and the spires it constantly occurs, although it is not encountered in the first and second stages, except in the modern tracery of the west window. The ball-flower is a fourteenth-century ornament: its constant use in the upper parts, contrasted with its total absence in the lower parts, supplies a very strong argument that a considerable time elapsed between the construction of the two lower stages and the upper. The very careful examination which took place when the whole front was lately restored revealed the fact that work was not proceeded with continuously; and by expert opinion the lowest stage is assigned to 1280, the next to 1300, while the upper stages are still later ; and perhaps the whole was not completed until well on into the last half of the fourteenth century.

As has been stated before, the present appearance of the west front is that of an entirely new building. In 1820 the front, which is said to have been then in a very dilapidated condition, was covered with Roman cement. So thoroughly was this done that the original stone facing only showed on the eastern side of the north-west tower. Careful drawings of the tracery there were made by Sir Gilbert Scott, and in 1877 the work of reconstructing was commenced. It took seven years, and the new west front was dedicated in 1884. Only five of the old statues remained, and it was decided to restore the others. There are in all one hundred and thirteen niches in the west front, including those on the north and south faces of the side turrets ; all but four are now filled, and about one hundred are in view of any one standing facing the middle of the front.

The large **West Window** has undergone several changes in its tracery; fortunately we have pictures showing all of them. In Fuller's "Church History" the tracery, as shown in Hollar's engraving, appears to be very simple. This tracery was all destroyed in the Civil Wars ; and that which replaced it at the Restoration was provided by James II., when Duke of York, but it was so ugly and unsuitable to the whole spirit of the cathedral that it was removed in 1869, and is now replaced by work which, though greatly differing from the original, yet preserves the spirit of fourteenth-century work. The Restoration window may be seen in the beautiful engraving in Britton's "Cathedral Antiquities."

There also is an engraving of the great west door as it was in the early part of the century, and before the Roman cement era of which mention has just been made. This doorway is one of the most beautiful in the country, has much in common with the "Prior's doorway" on the south side of Lincoln Cathedral. As Britton says : "Both are peculiarly rich and fanciful and calculated to excite the warmest admiration," but in his time the sculptured foliage and the figures running round the architrave mouldings and between the columns were so much battered and injured that it was almost impossible to tell the characters of some of them. This doorway is a recessed porch, the outer arch, in line with the main walls, being cusped and foliated with elaborate carving; the inner portion is divided into two arches; the whole being most elaborately decorated with carvings. The central clustered supports has a figure of the Virgin and Child, and on either side of the doorway, standing on clustered pillars beneath canopies, are figures of St. Mary Magdalene (on the north) with the box of ointment, and on the south, Mary the wife of Cleophas; farther forward on each side are vacant pedestals, and in the front are St. John the Evangelist (on the north) and St. Paul (on the south). Whether these were the characters originally represented is open to doubt; Stukeley suggested that what was left in his time represented the Virgin in the centre, and the four Evangelists with Moses and Aaron.

GREAT WEST DOORWAY IN 1813.

The **bas-relief figures** in the architrave already mentioned have been restored to represent the two genealogies of Christ as given by St. Matthew and St. Luke, on the north and south sides respectively, as follows:—

North side: Abraham, Isaac, Jacob, Boaz, Jesse, David, Virgin and Child.

South side: Adam, Seth, Enoch, Noah, Shem, Judah, and St. Joseph; the Virgin and St. Joseph being the two figures at the top of the arch.

There is a very beautiful fourteenth-century bas-relief above the central pillar of the doorway, representing Our Lord in Glory, with an angel on each side, having a serpent under his feet.

The doors are covered with fine iron work, which, with the exception of that on the lowest panel, is supposed to be original.

THE GREAT WEST DOORWAY.

The two side doorways in the west front are deeply recessed in three orders with very finely-carved mouldings. These also have bas-relief figures in the architraves. Those in the northern doorway represent the principal princes and princesses who promoted Christianity in England, while those in the southern doorway represent the leading early missionaries to England.

In the northern doorway, on the north side, are Ethelbert, Edwin, Oswald, Oswy, Peada, Wulphere; and on the south side, Bertha, Ethelburga, Hilda, Eanfled, Ermenilda, Werburga.

In the southern doorway, on the north side, are St. Aidan, Finan, Diuma, Ceollach, Trumhere, Jaruman; and on the south side, Gregory, Augustine, Paulinus, Theodore, Cuthbert, Wilfrid.

The corbels of the arches of these two doorways are interesting. Those of the north-west doorway represent Night on one side and the Morning Star on the other. The former is a female face with a reversed torch, and the Greek word NYX for night; the latter is a beautiful boy's face with a burning torch.

Those on the south-west doorway are a blindfolded face and an open face, representing the Law and the Gospel respectively.

Up to the time of the recent restoration a large statue of Charles II., who, by gifts of money and also of timber from Needham Forest, helped Bishop Hacket in the general repair after the Civil Wars, occupied the principal canopy in the middle of the central gable of the west front. This statue was the work of a certain stone-mason named William Wilson, who, by marrying a rich widow, "arrived at knighthood" in 1681. The statue, which certainly was not a work of art from all account of it, was taken down, and the pedestal is now occupied by a figure of Our Lord. The two other large canopied niches in the gable being filled with statues of Moses and Elijah, on the north and south sides respectively; while the four smaller statues represent, on the north, St. Gabriel, with St. Uriel underneath; and on the south, St. Michael, with St. Raphael below.

In giving the list of the statuary on the west front, which now follows, it is only necessary to say that there is no pretence that the characters now chosen were those originally represented.

All that could be done in filling the niches was to study the plan of other similar façades, such as that at Wells, and to imitate the general idea. Tradition, however, had it that the

Photochrom Co. Ltd., Photo.]
THE SOUTHERN DOORWAY OF THE WEST FRONT.

long row of figures in the top of the lowest stage represented the Saxon and English kings, with St. Chad in the centre, and the tradition has been respected.

The following is a list of all the statues not already

mentioned on the west front, including these on the north and south faces of the flanking turrets. The statues are enumerated in rows from the north side to the south.

On the northern tower the highest tier commences round the corner with two of the old figures already mentioned, then Aaron, Samuel, Hannah, another old figure, Deborah, Rachel, another old figure, Sarah, another old figure, and Eve.

On the southern tower the highest tier commences with Adam, Abel, Abraham, Isaac, Jacob, Melchisedec, Enoch, Methuselah, Noah, Daniel, Job, and Shem (these two last being, of course, round the corner on the south side).

Taking next the two rows on the northern tower to the north of the great west window, there are in the higher row, St. Editha, David, St. Helena, Solomon, St. Gabriel, Zechariah, Nahum, Amos, Jeremiah ; and in the lower row, Dean Bickersteth, St. Mark, Queen Victoria, St. Luke, St. Uriel, Malachi, Habakkuk, Obadiah, Daniel (Jeremiah being just above Daniel, by the window).

Taking next the two rows on the southern tower to the south of the great west window, there are in the higher row, Isaiah, Hosea, Jonah, Zephaniah, St. Michael, Bishop Hacket, Bishop Lonsdale, Bishop Selwyn (the niche round the corner is vacant), and in the lower row, Ezekiel, Joel, Micah, Haggai, St. Raphael, Bishop Clinton, Bishop Patteshall, Bishop Langton (the niche round the corner is vacant).

Next again below is the long row of kings with St. Chad in the centre stretching right across the cathedral, the pre-Conquest kings on the south side of St. Chad, the post-Conquest on the north, as follows :—William the Conqueror, William Rufus, Henry I., Stephen, Henry II., Richard I., John, Henry III., Edward I., Edward II., Edward III., Richard II., St. Chad, Peada, Wulphere, Ethelred, Offa, Egbert, Ethelwolf, Ethelbert, Ethelred, Alfred, Edgar, Canute, Edward the Confessor.

Lastly, there is the lowest row, which is broken three times by the doors ; these are St. Cyprian, St. Bartholomew, St. Simon, St. James the Less, St. Thomas (then the northern door), St. Philip, St. Andrew (then the central door with its seven niches and five statues already described), St. Paul, St. Matthew (then the southern door), St. James the Greater, St. Jude, St. Stephen, St. Clement, St. Werburga.

There is also a small figure of St. Antony over the belfry window on the south side.

A tour of the cathedral, starting by the north side, leads past the nave with its buttresses and flying-buttresses looking picturesque in their unrestored state, and there can be seen outside the seventh bay of the nave the remains of the entrance to Dean Yotton's chantry. Coming to the front of the north transept, it will be noticed that the doorway has steps inside leading down into the cathedral, while on the opposite side it will be found that the steps lead from the south door down outside; the level of the ground on the two sides of the cathedral being very different.

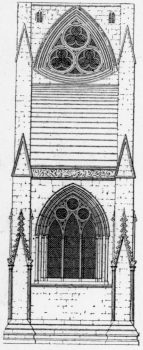

A BAY OF THE NAVE— EXTERIOR.

The North Doorway is extremely fine, and is deeply recessed. Like the other two main doorways of the cathedral,—that at the west end and that in the south transept—this doorway is double, the main arch being divided into two. The archivolts of these are lancet-shaped and covered with foliage, but not foliated as in the west door. Outside the double-arched doorway proper, the architrave is divided into five principal and several smaller mouldings; the larger ones being very finely carved, as to two, the second and fourth, with intertwisted foliage and scroll work; and as to the other three, the inner, middle, and outer, with small lozenge-shaped plaques containing bas-relief figures. These figures in the inner moulding are angels, in the middle one probably they are patriarchs and prophets. In the outer one, on the left or eastern side, the figures show the genealogy of Christ, beginning with Jesse at the springing stone, and ending with the Virgin and Child near the crown; while on the right-hand side, opposite Jesse, is the figure of St. Chad baptising the sons of King Wulphere, and above, the Apostles from St. Matthias to St. Peter at the crown. The whole architrave is surmounted by a weather moulding in the form of a gable, with a recently executed cross in the style of the thirteenth century at the top. The pillars on each side of the doorway have finely carved capitals, and the outer pillars are separated by lines of dog-toothing. The central pillar is very graceful, and consists of four slender shafts with carved capitals.

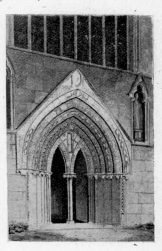

The whole forms a magnificent example of a doorway in the Early English style, but showing signs of its derivation from the Norman. There is a niche in the tympanum which was apparently in Britton's time empty; but it must soon after have been filled with an image of St. Anne in Roman cement; this has recently been replaced by a statue of the same saint by Mr W. R. Ingram, while above some Roman cement work in the top of the gable has been removed, and a vesica containing a bas-relief of Our Lord in Glory by Mr Bridgeman reproduces no doubt the original architect's idea. The doorway, though it has been considerably restored,

THE NORTH ENTRANCE IN 1813.

was not so much injured as a great deal of the rest of the cathedral, and so contains some very charming carving of the thirteenth century. There are two figures in Roman cement, one on each side of the doorway, representing St. Jude with a scroll, and St. James the Less with a club. No doubt these will both disappear before long, and their place be filled with modern statues.

Passing by the somewhat plain octagonal chapter-house, where we may perhaps wonder whether the small niches in the top of the buttresses which stick up like little turrets ever contained images, we come to the side of the choir and presbytery, which has not yet been restored, and then to the Lady Chapel.

The outside of the **Lady Chapel** has recently been very much altered ; and the old buttresses, which but the other day

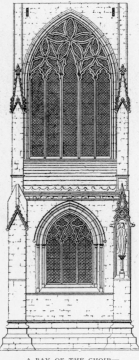

A BAY OF THE CHOIR—
EXTERIOR.

were as left by Bishop Langton, with only the hand of decay showing on them, are now gone, and in their place are brand new buttresses, with brand new niches and saints. Those in the top row are the holy women of the Old Testament, while below them are the holy women of the New Testament. The lower row represent Priscilla, Anna, Dorcas, Mary, Martha, Lydia, Phœbe and Elizabeth ; and above are Esther, Ruth, Naomi, Rizpah, Deborah, Miriam, Rachel, and Rebecca.

On the south side of the Lady Chapel are the curious chapels—known as the mortuary chapels—with their gabled fronts lying in the three spaces between the buttresses. These are more fully described in their place in the next chapter.

From this end of the cathedral can be well seen the arcaded parapet with its battlements, which runs round the top of the eastern half of the building and of the transepts, also the turrets of the sacristy with their high crocketted pinnacles ; from here, too, can be seen, what Professor Willis draws attention to, "that the rebuilt clerestory of the western part of the choir betrays by the lighter colour of its stone that it was a work subsequent to the eastern part." On one of the buttresses of the choir on this side is an ancient image of a female figure, but it is too much decayed to afford any clue to the character represented, though it remains a very charming instance of Gothic sculpture. On the east corner of the sacristy there is a modern figure of Godefroi de Bouillon, and at the other corner is a figure of St. Chad.

In the gable of the **South Transept** is a very beautiful rose

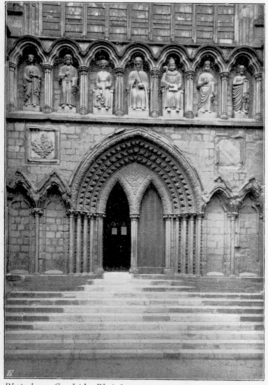

Photochrom Co. Ltd., Photo.]
DOORWAY OF SOUTH TRANSEPT BEFORE THE LAST RESTORATION.

window, which is hidden by the stone groining from the inside. Mr J. O. Scott, in a lecture already referred to, declared that "this rose window is so high up in the gable that it never could have been combined with any stone groining. But, by referring to York Minster, between which and Lichfield many curious parallels may be traced, it is seen at once how a rose window in this position may be brought into the general design. This is effected by using a particular kind of wooden groining, the part of which nearest to the gable wall is lifted up so as to exhibit the window from within the building."

The large doorway in the south transept, which as seen from the outside is at the top of a flight of steps, very much resembles the doorway on the north side, but the carving is not so fine ; it has been very much restored, and three shields have been in comparatively recent times carved in the tympanum. The shields show the arms of the see, of Bishop Lloyd, and Dean Addison, thus declaring this to have been done about 1700.

To the right of this doorway, outside the southern end of the transept aisle, is an ancient monument, probably of an archdeacon. A carved figure lies in a recess surmounted by a stone canopy.

The large heavy buttresses which disfigure the outside of this transept were the work of Wyatt at the end of the last century. The outside of the nave on this side presents a very different appearance to the other side. Here everything is new and uninteresting. The entrance to the bell tower is on this side, and a winding stair leads to the belfry stage.

There are ten **Bells,** seven of which date from about 1687, and are therefore of the same age as the bishop's palace. In that year Hacket's six bells, which can only have been hanging some sixteen or seventeen years, were found to be useless, and a subscription was raised to replace them with a peal of ten. There is a letter from the dean and chapter to Elias Ashmole, in which it is stated that Henry Bagley of Ecton, the bell-founder, had "so over-sized the eight bells he had cast, that they had swallowed up all the metal for the ten," and that eighty pounds more would be required, but that they did not regret the mistake as it "would make extremely for the advantage and glory of the cathedral (the bigness of such a ring far more befitting the place)." Only seven of these bells are now in use ; the other three are by Rudhall of Gloucester and Mears of London. In 1748 the belfry caught fire and the ninth bell cracked with the heat, but it was recast in the same year, and since then there has been no change.

The story of the earliest cathedral bells is lost. It was usual in early days to hang the bells in a separate tower somewhere in the cathedral precincts. Here, we know that in 1315 the bell tower was burnt down,—"Combustum fuit campanile cum campanis in clauso Lichfeldensi." The site of this tower was lately discovered in the bishop's garden. Dean Heywood, in 1477, gave a large bell to the cathedral—it was known as the Jesus Bell; the gift is mentioned in the *Cantaria Sancti Blasii*, where the cost is stated to be one hundred pounds. The bell bore this inscription:—

> "*I am the bell of Jesus, and Edward is our king,*
> *Sir Thomas Heywood first caused me to ring.*"

This bell was hung in the south-west tower, which thus came to be called the Jesus-Bell Tower. The bell was destroyed during the Civil Wars. An ancient writer quoted by Shaw, after detailing the terrible fates of those who took part against religious houses and churches, says: "Nor shall I relate what happened to one, Pickins, a pewterer, who on July 26, 1653, knoct in pieces the fair bell called Jesus, at Lichfield, he being the chief officer appointed for demolishing that cathedral."

There was also a bell called the "Clocke Bell," which was hung in the lowest storey of the Jesus spire. It is shown in the south view given in Fuller's "Church History," and particular attention is there directed to it. The clock bell and all the others are now hung in the top storey of the tower.

There is also a small bell in the great central tower called "the Tantony": it formerly belonged to the Dyott family.

In the south-west tower is also the new **Clock,** which was put up in 1890. The face is underneath, in the west end of the south aisle of the nave; there is no outside face. The well-known Cambridge quarter chimes can, it is said, be heard at a distance of three miles.

In the green grass of the close are many tombstones, and round about the cathedral stone coffins have been dug up; on the north side of the choir is the traditional burying-place of two Mercian kings.

CHAPTER III

LICHFIELD is one of the smallest cathedrals in England. In length it only measures 370 feet from the inside of the west door to the extreme end of the inside of the Lady Chapel, while the interior of the nave, with its aisles, is only a little more than 68 feet wide; and yet its smallness is not the first fact that will strike the visitor on entering the west door: rather, on the other hand, its immense length in proportion to its height and width will be noticed, but probably all other feelings will be forgotten in the beauty of the vista that lies before him. The long line of arches and the long low roof, with its almost countless bosses, lead the eye down to the Lady Chapel, where a mass of blue and red shows that the cathedral has some of the most beautiful glass in the kingdom.

The orientation of the nave and choir are not the same— the choir and Lady Chapel being considerably inclined to the north. Many have been the theories raised by the curious discoveries made as to the deflections of various parts of this cathedral. They are too numerous to quote here, and it will be sufficient to note that the total deflection of the east end from the true east is about ten degrees.

The Nave.—The view of the interior of the cathedral from the inside of the west door is, as we have said, extremely beautiful. This beauty is much enhanced by the general appearance of unity in the whole design. There seems to be no mixture of styles, and though a closer examination of the details of the interior shows that there is a very marked difference between the style in which the nave is built and that which was in vogue when the Lady Chapel and presbytery were erected; yet the whole, having been built at a time when the Early English style was giving

54

place gradually to the Decorated, or, in the more eastern portion, when that later style was well established, the general effect of the cathedral, seen from this aspect, is one of unity. The exact date of the nave cannot be determined, and there is no direct evidence on which to base a theory; but it is very clear, from a comparison of its style with that of churches whose history is known, that it must have been commenced and carried to a speedy conclusion about the middle of the thirteenth century. Professor Willis gives the date as 1250, and other archæologists at various dates between that and 1280. There is no doubt, at anyrate, that it was built at the transitional period of the Early English style, and it would be described by some as belonging to the Early Decorated period, and by others as belonging to the geometrical period of the Decorated style. The nave, including the western front, consists of eight bays, having aisles on the north and south sides, with the same number of bays; but the spaces underneath the two western towers are considerably larger than the other aisle bays, though not large enough to be looked upon as western transepts, as is possible in some churches where there is a similar arrangement. Many writers have complained of the insufficient height of the nave, and that the general effect is thereby spoilt, and to a very limited extent this may be true.

A BAY OF THE NAVE—
INTERIOR.

Probably the nave roof was at one time of much higher pitch; the course on the outside of the great tower suggests it, as also does the fact that the great west window runs into the roof. Probably the roof was lowered when the presbytery was built, and the

whole roofing of the cathedral brought down to the same
level.

The piers are large, and consist of clustered shafts, lozenge-
shaped in plan, set on much moulded bases, and having

beautifully carved foliated capitals
from which spring architrave mouldings of great variety. From the
base and up the centre of each
pier runs a cluster of three fine
columns to capitals, also foliated, at
the top of the triforium ; from these
spring five vaulting ribs, three of
which diverge to an ornamental
central rib, and two to a small
similarly decorated transverse rib.
There are finely carved bosses at
the intersection of all the various
ribs. The top of each arch touches
the string course, above which is the
beautiful triforium. This consists of
a row of double arches, each arch
being sub-divided into two lights
with geometrical tracery above. The
mouldings are highly decorated with
dog-toothing, and the string course
between the triforium and the clerestory, as well as the moulding enclosing the clerestory windows, has this
same ornament, which is freely used
and produces a very rich effect.
The clerestory windows are spherical
triangles enclosing three circles with
quatrefoil cusps ; the form of these
windows is somewhat rare, but similar
windows are to be seen at West-

A BAY OF THE CHOIR—
INTERIOR.

minster, Hereford, Carlisle, and York. The spandrels of most of
the pier arches are ornamented with a large circle with five cusps,
across which the vault shafts pass ; this decoration will be seen
again in the choir. A notable feature in these bays is the
size of the triforium in proportion to the size of the pier arches
and clerestory ; this gives it unusual importance in the general

THE NAVE IN 1813.

scheme.   At Lincoln, where there is a similar triforium, a very different effect is produced by its comparative smallness.   The open tracery here is very much like that in Westminster Abbey.

Photochrom Co. Ltd., Photo.
THE NAVE, LOOKING EAST.

It will be seen that the dripstones of the arches and windows terminate in small sculptured heads : a usual arrangement at this period.   It may be added that the beautiful capitals have scarcely been restored at all ; so little damage had been done to them, that when the whitewash was removed during the recent restorations, they were found to have been hardly touched either by decay, Puritans, or previous restorers.

The roof of the nave was greatly damaged at the time of the Civil Wars—indeed, it has been said that the central spire, in its fall, completely smashed it in ; but this is probably not the case, as the spire almost certainly fell on the other side of the tower.   Still, it is not difficult, after reading an account of the siege, to understand that the roof would be much injured. About a century after its repair by Bishop Hacket, it was found that the great weight of the stone groining was forcing out the clerestory walls, already much weakened by rough usage, and, in consequence, Wyatt removed the stone work in several bays, and replaced it with lath and plaster work made to imitate the rest of the roofing.   Sir Gilbert Scott was urged to restore the old stone vaulting, but he decided that without great structural alterations, principally to the buttresses, which he did not feel justified in making, this could not be done.   The vaulting has been coloured so that the difference between the stone compartments—the most eastern and the two western ones—and the plaster compartments might not be noticed ; it will easily be seen how much the clerestory walls have been thrust out.   It is also interesting to note that at about the same time Wyatt restored the roof of the aisles to its old pitch. Originally, as now, the aisle roof ascended so as to reach to just below the clerestory windows.   In Hollar's picture the upper portion of the triforium windows can be seen, so that they must have become practically a portion of the clerestory during this time.   Investigation of the windows themselves proves that they have been glazed, and this confirms what otherwise, considering the great inexactness of the pictures of the period, could not be inferred with certainty.   There is a view of the cathedral as late as 1781 showing this arrangement ; but in Jackson's "History of Lichfield," 1796, the aisle roof hides the whole of the triforium as at present.

The windows of the aisles agree well with the other windows of the nave, and have three lights with trefoiled circles in the head, while below the windows is an arcade resting on a bench, the arches of which are surmounted with pediments richly carved.   There are six of these arches in each bay, and between the bays rise triple vaulting shafts with carved capitals of leafage ;

from these spring three ribs running to a central rib on which are beautiful bosses like those in the nave.

The Great West Window.—The tracery of this window

Photochrom Co. Ltd., Photo.]
THE NAVE, LOOKING WEST.

has already been discussed in the description of the exterior. The present glass was placed there in 1869, to the memory of Canon Hutchinson, who, perhaps, of all was most eager for the restoration of the cathedral, and to whose untiring energy, it is said, is due the wholesale renovation of the interior by Sir Gilbert Scott. This window was the result of a public subscription, and is the work of Messrs Clayton & Bell. The six large figures represent St. Michael, St. Joseph, St. Mary, and the Three Magi, while underneath are small pictures of the Annunciation, the Angel warning Joseph, the Nativity, the Journey of the Magi, the Magi inquire of Herod, and the Flight into Egypt. As to the previous glass in this window, there seems to be no record of that which must have decorated it before the Civil Wars. In Shaw's "History of Staffordshire," there are long lists of the glass to be found in the cathedral; but it is difficult to decide which window is being described. After the Restoration, we have in a Bodleian MS. the following record :—" Oct. 6, 1671. Arms in the Great West Window, Arms of King Charles the Second, Crest and Supporters; Arms of James Duke of York, his brother, Crest and Supporters. And beneath them, *Serenissimus princeps Jacobus dux Ebor hanc fenestram. F.F.*" Britton says it was afterwards filled with painted glass, the work of Brookes, by the legacy of Dr Addenbroke, who died dean of this cathedral in 1776.

Over the great west door in the inside of the cathedral was formerly inscribed :—

> *Oswyus est Lichfield fundator, sed reparator*
> *Offa fuit ; regum fama perennis erit :*
> *Rex Stephanus, rex Henricus primusque Richardus,*
> *Rex et Johannis, plurima dona dabant.*
>
> *Pene haec millenos ecclesia floruit annos,*
> *Duret ad extremum nobilis usque diem,*
> *Daque deus longum, ut floreat hae sacra aedes*
> *Et celebret nomen plebs ibi sancta tuum.*
> *Fundata est ecclesia Merciencis*
> *Quae nunc Lichfieldia dicitur*
> *Facta Cathedralis*
> *Anno Domini*
> *DCLVII*

Dugdale, in his "Visitation of Staffordshire," gives us this inscription. It has long since disappeared. Pennant mentions a curious or, as he calls it, "droll" epitaph on the

floor near the west door, but there is no sign of it now :—
" *William Roberts of Overbury, some time malster in this
town (tells you) for the love I bore to choir service, I chose
to be buried in this place.* He died Decr. 16th, 1768."

From a MS. quoted by Shaw we learn that before the
Great War "on a fair marble gravestone, placed on the
right-hand at the entrance into the choir, is this inscription
on a brass plate :—

" *Here lyeth George Bullen lat dean of this church who made
his own epitaph—viz.,*

> *Lo here in earth my body lyes,*
> *Whose sinfull lyfe deserves the rod :*
> *Yet I believe the same shall rise,*
> *And praise the mercies of my God.*
> *As for my soule let none take thought,*
> *It is with him that hath it bought ;*
> *For God on me doth mercy take*
> *For nothing else but Jhesus sake.*"

Bullen or Boleyn was dean during the greater part of the
reign of Elizabeth, who offered him the bishopric of Worcester,
which he refused. Elizabeth, it will be remembered, was
the daughter of Anne Boleyn, whose kinsman the dean was.

The Font stands between the first and second pillars
from the west door on the north side of the nave. It is
quite modern, and is the gift of the Honourable Mrs Henry
Howard, widow of the late dean. It is made of alabaster and
Caen stone, and is supported on marble pillars. There are
four sculptured panels in relief, representing—"The Entry
into the Ark," "The Passage of the Red Sea," "The Baptism
of our Lord," and "The Resurrection." Between these there
are niches containing figures of St. Mary, St. Peter, St. Chad,
and St. Helen.

A curious old font was discovered in 1856 immediately
under the place where the present altar stands. It was very
simple in form, being about a yard and a half square and
two feet thick, with a hemispherical cavity in it. It had
been coloured bright red, and was much cracked, as though
it had been subjected to intense heat. How it came where
it was is not known. It may have been discarded as rubbish
or hidden as a relic.

The Pulpit is in the nave, and is fixed to the north-western pier of the tower. Its design and execution were by Sir Gilbert Scott and Mr Skidmore respectively, who were also responsible for the choir screen. The pulpit is of wrought-iron, brass, copper, enamels, and marble. In the middle there is a bronze group representing St. Peter preaching on the Day of Pentecost. There are stairs on each side of the pulpit. The brass **Lectern** is also modern, and is in the usual form of an eagle. It was presented by the members of the Lichfield

Photochrom Co. Ltd., Photo.]
NORTH AISLE OF NAVE, LOOKING EAST

Theological College, and was executed by Mr Hardman of Birmingham. The **Litany Desk** is by Messrs Rattee & Kett of Cambridge, the well-known carvers ; and the **Bishop's Chair**, which stands under the great tower, was presented by the clergy of Derbyshire when that county was transferred from this diocese to the new diocese of Southwell. The chair is not of striking beauty.

In the **North Aisle of the Nave** there are several monuments and some modern glass. The window in the north-west tower has recently been adorned with glass to the memory of Bishop Lonsdale, under whom the recent restoration commenced. The subject is "The Presentation of Christ in the Temple," and it is the work of Messrs Burlison & Grylls. Close to this is a tablet, originally placed in the north transept by order of Ann Seward, who had considerable fame as a poetess in the last century, to the memory of her father, Canon Seward, his wife and daughter Sarah. It also commemorates her own death. The lines are by Sir Walter Scott, but it is impossible to be enthusiastic over them. They end—

> "*Honour'd, beloved, and mourn'd here Seward lies;*
> *Her worth, her warmth of heart, our sorrows say,—*
> *Go seek her genius in her living lay.*"

There is a representation of the poetess mourning her dead relatives, while her harp is hanging neglected on a tree. On the other side is a memorial tablet to Lady Mary Wortley Montagu, who was a native of Lichfield. In these days of anti-vaccination agitations it is interesting to read the inscription which runs:—

> "*The Rt. Honourable Lady Mary Wortley Montagu, who happily introduced from Turkey into this country the Salutary Art of inoculating the Smallpox. Convinced of its efficacy, she first tried it with success on her own children, and then recommended the practice of it to her fellow-citizens. Thus, by her example and advice, we have softened the Virulence and escaped the danger of this Malignant Disease. To perpetuate the memory of such benevolence, and to express the gratitude for the benefit she hereby has received from this Alleviating Art, this Monument is erected by Henrietta Inge, Relict of Theodore William Inge, Esq., and Daughter of Sir John Wrotesley, Baronet. In the year of Our Lord, 1789.*"

Close at hand is a tablet in memory of Mr Gilbert Walmesley, who was registrar of the diocese, and an early and close friend of Dr Johnson. Of him the latter wrote, in his life of Edmund Smith (one of the well-known "Lives of the Poets"), that passage which contains the celebrated sentence about David Garrick so often quoted. Speaking of Gilbert

E

Walmesley, he says that he is "not able to name a man of equal knowledge. His acquaintance with books was great; such was his amplitude of learning, and such his copiousness of communication, that it may be doubted whether a day now passes in which I have not some advantage from his friendship. At this man's table I enjoyed many cheerful and instructive hours with companions such as are not often found; with one who has lengthened, and one who has gladdened life; with Dr James, whose skill in physic will be long remembered, and with David Garrick, whose death has eclipsed the gaiety of nations, and impoverished the public stock of harmless pleasure."

There are other monuments in this aisle, but they are scarcely of such general interest. Here are tablets in memory of Jane and Catherine Jervis and of Elizabeth and Arabella Buchanan. There is a stained glass window by Messrs Burlison & Grylls containing three large figures of Joshua, St. Michael, and the Centurion, with, underneath, pictures of the Angel appearing to Joshua, the Centurion at the Cross, and the Centurion coming to Our Lord; above, in the tracery of the window, are angels. This window was the gift of the officers of the 38th (1st Staffordshire) Regiment; on one side are their Peninsular, and on the other their Crimean colours, which the dean and chapter received from the regiment with much ceremony in 1886 and 1887 respectively. Beneath the window is a brass in memory of those members of the regiment who died in the Peninsula, first Burmah, Crimean, and Egyptian (1882) wars, and the Indian Mutiny. There are also brasses to Lieutenant-Colonels Sinclair and Eyre and the officers and men of this regiment who fell in the first Soudan war, and also brasses to Colonel Bromley Davenport and Sir Arthur Scott, Bart. Here, too, is a window in memory of Canon Madan, his wife and children : the subject being Faith, Hope, and Charity. In the window next the transept is some quite new glass in memory of Canon Curteis, the large figures representing Samuel, St. Paul, and Origen, while below are Samuel teaching the Sons of the Prophets, St. Paul saying farewell to the Elders at Miletus, and St. Catherine and the Philosophers of Alexandria.

The famous Dr Stukeley, writing about 1715, says : "As you walk down the north aisle, by a little doorway, formerly a chapel, where lay several figures now demolished, yet one remains, who was dean Yotton, his coat of arms at his head and Yot with a tun by it which shows his name." The only remaining sign of this chapel is the entrance, which can be plainly seen from the outside of the cathedral.

In the **South Aisle of the Nave,** at the west end, there is a monument to Dean Addison, the father of the great essayist and poet ; he died in 1703. His memorial slab is now under the Jesus Tower, but formerly it was on the north of the west door. The glass in the window of the tower is in memory of Dean Howard, during whose time as dean so much of the work of restoration was done, and who so munificently aided the work. This glass, which is by Messrs Burlison & Grylls, represents St. Michael and the Dragon, and St. Chad. The other glass on this side is the window of the fifth bay, by Messrs Clayton & Bell, the subjects being Our Lord and Lazarus, Our Lord and Mary and Martha, and Mary Magdalene washing Our Lord's feet ; in the next bay the glass, by Messrs Ward & Hughes, shows Faith, Hope, and Charity ; in the seventh bay the glass is by Messrs Clayton & Bell, and has David and Goliath for its subject, and is in memory of the officers of the 64th (2nd Staffordshire) Regiment who fell in the Indian Mutiny. There is in the eighth bay a window by Hardman in memory of Helen, wife of Josiah Spode. Between the aisle and the nave there is a brass in the floor in memory of the late Earl of Lichfield, placed there in 1854. There are several other modern brasses and tablets.

In this aisle are two of the three semi-effigies to be seen in the cathedral. These show only the heads and the feet. Britton says : "They are said to represent two old canons of the church ; and are evidently of ancient date, as they appear to have been placed in the present situation at the time of building or finishing the nave." One of these is in a better state of preservation than the other, and shows in the drapery the remains of colour.

The Transepts are earlier than the nave in style, having been built in the beginning of the thirteenth century : the south transept first, and then the north. It must have been for these transepts that Henry III., in 1235 and 1238, granted licences to the dean and chapter of Lichfield to dig stone from the royal forest of Hopwas for the new fabric of the

church of Lichfield.   Whether these ecclesiastics did more
harm than the king liked in digging on the first occasion
cannot be said, but on the second occasion they are permitted "fodere petram ad fabricam ecclesiae suae de Liche-
feld in quarrera de Hopwas ; ita tamen quod hoc fiat sine
detrimento forestae nostrae "—that is to say, they were to do as
little damage as possible.

The transepts have three bays each, with eastern aisles,
the aisle belonging to the north transept being very much the
larger.   There can be no doubt that when the Norman transepts were standing there were no aisles ; nor were any contemplated when the choir was built, for, as Professor Willis

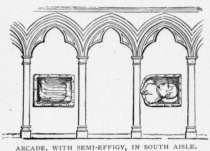

says : "The side walls
of the choir are con-
tinued to the transepts,
and had windows in the
part looking into the
present transept aisles.
Probably when the
choir was built Norman
transepts were standing,
and had each an apsidal
chapel looking east in
the usual manner."

ARCADE, WITH SEMI-EFFIGY, IN SOUTH AISLE.

The history of the
roof is extremely interesting.   We know that "in 1243 King
Henry III. issued a commission to Walter Grey, Archbishop
of York, to expedite the works at St. George's Chapel,
Windsor, in which he orders a lofty wooden roof, like the
roof of the new work at Lichfield, to appear like stone
work, with good ceiling (*celatura ?*) and painting.   The transepts of Lichfield have now stone vaults, considerably later
than the walls, and, therefore, may have had a wooden vault
at first.   The date would suit the transepts better than the
choir, and it may be remarked that the early abacus of the
vault shaft (at least, in the south transept) is surmounted by a
second abacus in the Perpendicular style, which shows the
later construction of the springing stones of the present stone
vault."   The low stone vaulting has destroyed the effect which
the original windows in the north and south ends of the
transepts must have produced.   At the south end was probably

a large five-light Early English window, surmounted by a rose window. The rose window still remains, but, being above the present groining, cannot be seen from inside the cathedral; the five lights are replaced by a nine-light obtuse-headed window, which seems much too large for the transept; and this effect is increased by the extreme whiteness and transparency of its glass. At the north end, the five-light window is surmounted with three small lights, but these last again are hidden in the roof.

The windows in the transepts have seen many changes, and are now mostly in the Perpendicular manner, the exceptions being in the west wall of the south transept, and the north window just referred to. Until 1892 this was a large Perpendicular window—which, though early, and prior to the Civil War, was a manifest intrusion on the space originally occupied by an Early English window. The old design, which is not unlike that of the famous window at York, has again taken its place. Canon Lonsdale says that this change is "in every sense a restoration: for, on taking out the Perpendicular window, and removing such of the stone work as was defective on either side, the headings of the five Early English lights, which had unquestionably composed the original window, were dis-

DETAIL OF A SEMI-EFFIGY.

covered, hidden away by the later workmen. The cusps, or headings, of the lights, as they are now seen from the inside, are, with the exception of six stones, the very identical material which the Early English builders carved, and placed in that spot. Of these six missing stones, three have since been discovered during the work going on in the south transept."

There can be no doubt that some of the Perpendicular work in the cathedral is due to the general repair at the Restoration;

but Professor Willis declares that many of the changes are earlier, and that they were perhaps effected in the time between Bishops Heyworth and Blythe, 1420 to 1503. The engravings of Hollar, already referred to, were published before 1660, and show Perpendicular windows in the gable of the south transept and in the clerestory; and though from these pictures nothing can be gleaned about the north transept, the character of the Perpendicular work was such that it also, as has just been stated, must have been prior to the Rebellion. It is possible, on the outside western face of the north transept, to trace the old lancet windows, which must have been arranged in groups of three, while the lower windows on the west side of the south transept are still in their old form, though on this side there are only two lancets to each bay. It may be mentioned here that underneath these last windows, on the outside, there is an arcading with simple pointed arches which does not appear on the other transept. Inside the arcading differs in the two transepts; in the south and older one the pointed arches are plain, while on the north they are cusped. This arcading is almost entirely new; what there was of it until recently was principally of plaster.

From the ground plan of this cathedral published by Browne Willis in 1727, we see that the whole of the aisle of the north transept is described as "The Bishop's Consistory Court and St. Stephen's Chapel," while the aisle of the south transept is divided into two parts, the southern being called "The Dean's Consistory Court," the northern "The Vicar's Vestry." St. Stephen's Chapel was in the inner bay of the aisle; and it has been suggested that "the chantry of St. Anne and the image of Jesus" was in the rood loft of the same transept.

In the **North Transept** are many memorial tablets, but it cannot be said that they are of general interest either from their beauty, age, or on account of the eminence of the persons commemorated. On the west side of the steps down from the north door is the curious monument to Dean Heywood, who died in 1492, and whose benefactions are mentioned in their proper places. The monument is sadly decayed, but there is a print of it in Shaw's "Staffordshire," taken, says Britton, from Dugdale's "Visitation." From this we know that the upper part is now missing; the lower part, which remains, shows the skeleton of the dean—his body after death—while above was his representation in full canonical costume. Similar monuments may be seen at St. John's College, Cambridge, in the chapel, and at Exeter and Lincoln Cathedrals. On the other side of the door is a large modern monument to Archdeacon Iles, who died in 1888 : the figure is recumbent. Above the door is a marble tablet to Dean Woodhouse ; he gave the glass— now in the Guildhall—which filled the Perpendicular window recently replaced by the present Early English window. The new glass, and indeed the new window, was given by Mr James Chadwick of Hints Hall, near Tamworth ; it is known as the Jesse window, and gives the genealogy of our Lord according to St. Matthew. The figures beginning from the west side represent (1) Achaz, Asa, Abia ; (2) Ezekias, Solomon, Roboam ; (3) the Virgin Mary and Child, Salathiel, David, Jesse ; (4) Josias, Josaphat, Joram ; (5) Manasses, Joatham, Ozias ; with angels in the four side lights. The inscription under the window says : " Hanccine fenestram Jacobus Chadwick de vico Hints reficiendam vitroque picto ornandam impensis suis curavit. A.D. MDCCCXCIII." Messrs Clayton & Bell are responsible for this window.

The whole of the aisle of this transept is taken up with the organ, in front of which a metal screen or gryll was placed in 1881 by the officers and men of the 80th Regiment, in memory of their comrades who fell in the Zulu War. The screen is ornamented with imitations of Zulu shields and assegais. There are many tablets in this aisle, but they are entirely hidden by the organ.

The Organ was presented by Mr Spode of Hawkesyard Park, near Lichfield, in 1860, and was first used at the reopening in 1861 ; in 1884 it needed repair, and was then very much enlarged by Messrs Hill & Son, the well-known organbuilders of London, the expense being defrayed by voluntary subscriptions. It was dedicated, at the same time as the restored west front, in the presence of a vast concourse of people, on May 29th, 1884. The console of the organ is now behind the stalls in the first bay of the south aisle of the choir. It is interesting to learn from Canon Lonsdale that, when it was found necessary to build an engine-house in the close to supply motive power to the organ, in digging out the chamber, somewhat to the east of the steps leading to the north door, two or three cannon balls and the remains of a shell were unearthed at a short distance from the surface.

The present organ is the successor to many other organs. The first of which there is any record was given to the cathedral by Dean Heywood, as is known from this entry in the *Cantaria S. Blasii*, in the cathedral library : " Magna organa in pulpito . Item cito post festum nativitatis Sancti Johannis Baptiste . Anno domini MCCCC . octogesimo secundo . ex providencia et sumptibus magistri Thome Heywode decani antedicti . conferuntur ecclesi cath lich organa nova magnae quantitatis . et formae decentis . ad honorem sancti cedde et ornamentum ecclesiae precij xxvi.Li. iij.s. iiij.d. totalitur de sumptibus et expensis predicti decani . Sma xxvj.Li. iij.s. iiij.d."

Dean Heywood also presented another organ, which was known as the Jesus organ; but it was much smaller presumably, as it cost rather less than half as much.

The next time there is mention of an organ is in 1634, when, in an account of their travels by three tourists, they say : " The organs and voices were deep and sweet, their anthems we were much delighted with, and of the voyces, 2 Trebles, 2 Counter-tenors, and 2 Bases, that equally on each side of the Quire most melodiously acted and performed their parts."

The organ here referred to, however "deep and sweet," was not considered good enough, for in 1636, according to a deed still preserved in the cathedral, the dean and chapter purchased an organ from Robert Dallam of Covent Garden, which, no doubt, "was the pair of organs valued at £200 " destroyed by the Puritans.   The organ that Hacket set up was obtained by the subscriptions of ladies ; the bishop writes : "An Organ is bespoke at £600 price, to be call'd the Ladies Organ, because none but the honourable and most pious of that sex shall contribute to that sum."   The names of the chief subscribers were written on the organ : " Illustrissima heroina Francisca ducissima Somersetensis.   Honoratissima domina, comitissa Devon : Clarissima domina, Jana, domina de Gerard Bromley," and many others, as set out by Ashmole, who also tells us that there were "coats of arms under the organ at the entrance into the choir," showing that the organ loft was situated between the two eastern piers of the tower.   Harwood, in his " History of Lichfield," tells us of another organ "which was removed in A.D. 1740 to the vicar's hall, and became at length an ornament to Mr Greene's museum," whence it afterwards found its way to the church at Hamstall Ridware. While in the vicar's hall it was damaged by soldiers quartered there in the '45. It is now in the bishop's palace. In 1740 it was replaced in the cathedral by an organ by Schwarbrook, which in turn, in Wyatt's time, was superseded by one by Samuel Green—this was much larger, and took up the whole of the western bay of the choir. The present organ is much the largest the cathedral has possessed, and, compared to the old one in the palace, is so large that, according to Mr Hewitt, the whole of the latter would go inside the pedal pipes of the former.

The south transept has its full share of monuments, two of which are of great interest. These are the memorials to Dr Johnson and to his friend, David Garrick, the actor. The busts are both by Sir Richard Westmacott, R.A. The inscription to the first says :

The Friends of Samuel Johnson, LL.D. (a native of Lichfield), erected this Monument as a tribute of respect to the Memory of a man of extensive learning, a distinguished Moral Writer, and a Sincere Christian. He died the 13th of December 1784 ; Aged 75 years.

The other reads :

EVA MARIA, Relict of DAVID GARRICK, Esq., caused this Monument to be erected to the Memory of her beloved Husband, who died the 20th January 1779 : Aged 63 years.

Garrick had not only the amiable qualities of private life, but such astonishing dramatic talents as to well verify the observations of his friend : " His death eclipses the gaiety of nations, and impoverishes the public stock of harmless pleasure."

Samuel Johnson was born in Lichfield, where his father was a bookseller ; his shop is still standing, scarcely altered, on the west side of the Market Place, close to the monument of his famous son (see p. 136). David Garrick came with his parents to live in Lichfield when very young, and he and Johnson attended the Grammar School together. There was a difference of several years in their ages, but their life-long friendship must have begun early, seeing that Johnson wrote the Prologue for Garrick's performance of Farquhar's comedy, "The Recruiting Officer," which took place at the Bishop's Palace when Garrick was only eleven years old. Some years after, when Johnson had left Oxford and had set up a school in the neighbourhood of Lichfield, Garrick joined him as a pupil; but the venture did not prove successful, and master and pupil left Lichfield for London, where each in his own line reached the highest summit of fame.

These memorials stand side by side in the aisle; for some reason, the busts were removed to the library when the interior was being restored by Sir Gilbert Scott, but they have once again been replaced in the spot originally chosen for them. The friendship of Johnson and Garrick was long and cordial: it is fitting we should see that in their death they were not divided.

In this aisle, which until recently was used as the Dean's Consistory Court, is another monument by Westmacott; this is in memory of Andrew Newton, who was so munificent a friend to his native Lichfield. He founded the institution on the west side of the close for the widows and orphans of clergymen, which he also endowed; and on his death, in 1806, he left a library of books to the cathedral.

In the first bay of the aisle is a monument to the officers and men of the 80th Regiment (Staffordshire Volunteers). The design is Egyptian, and is surmounted by a sphinx. Over the monument hang colours taken from the Sikhs, and on the wall behind are the old regimental colours. At the south end is a very fine and costly altar tomb—to Admiral Sir William Parker, who, when he died in 1866, was the last survivor of Nelson's captains. The slab of Pyrenean jasper is inlaid with a gold cross, and the front is adorned with stones of porphyry and lapis lazuli. The window above has some of the Herkenrode glass left over from the Lady Chapel, together with some modern glass. The great south window, which, as has just been stated, is in the Perpendicular style, was in 1895 adorned with new glass; this was the gift of Mr A. P. Heywood-Lonsdale, in memory of his father and his uncle, Bishop Lonsdale. The subject is "I am the vine, ye are the branches," and represents Our Lord in the centre surrounded by angels, with the principal bishops of the Early Christian Church. The six early British bishops: St. Columba, Scotland; St. Wulstan, Worcester; St. Chad, Lichfield; St. Augustine, Canterbury; St. Aidan, Northumbria; St. Hugh, Lincoln, are at the feet of Our Lord. The other bishops are St. Basil, Caesarea; St. Cyril, Jerusalem; St. Patrick, Ireland; St. Ignatius,

Antioch ; St. Polycarp, Smyrna ; St. Boniface, Germany ; St. Martin, Tours ; St. David, Wales ; St. Gregory, Rome ; St. Augustine, Hippo ; St. Athanasius, Alexandria ; St. Cyprian, Carthage ; St. Isidore, Spain ; St. Chrysostom, Constantinople ; St. Ambrose, Milan ; and St. Vigilius, Arles. This glass is by Mr C. E. Kempe. On the west side are several brasses and tablets, including one to John Saville, vicar choral of the cathedral, who died in 1803. The lines underneath are by the Miss Seward whose own memorial is in the north aisle of the nave ; they, like so much of the elegiac poetry of the period, owe not only their style, but a good many of their phrases, to the poet Gray.

The Choir, with the presbytery and retro-choir—that is to say, the whole extent of that part of the cathedral between the central tower and the entrance to the Lady Chapel—has eight bays. The most noticeable difference between it and the nave, is the absence of a triforium. Professor Willis says : "The entire height of the severey (or bay) is divided into two nearly equal parts, of which the lower is given to the pier arches, the upper to the clerestory. The window-sills of the latter are high, and there is a passage in front of them immediately above the table-ment or string course over the pier arches. This passage, the veritable triforium, pierces the great piers of masonry which sustain the vault. The high sills receive the sloping roof of the side aisles, and have three plain open arches in each severey to air the roof." These sills are panelled with a foliated arcading, and in front of the passage there is an open trefoil work parapet. The effect of the windows inside is much enhanced by the lovely quatrefoil ornamentation with which their splays are decorated. In the single window—the east on the south side—where the original tracery remains, it is very beautiful and graceful, and is a good example of the Decorated period ; but into the other windows Perpendicular tracery has been introduced.

The vaulting is very much the same as in the nave, but the vaulting shafts divide into seven instead of five ribs. The bosses, as everywhere else in the cathedral, are very deeply and richly carved.

On the four eastern sets of piers long slender shafts run up from the base of the piers in the same way as in the nave, and similarly the spandrels are ornamented with foliated circles, of which nearly all trace had disappeared before the recent restoration. This, however, is not the arrangement on the three western pairs. It was found here that these shafts did not reach the ground; and so Sir Gilbert Scott, having discovered a portion of the sculptured wing of an angel just above the dean's present stall, decided upon finishing the shafts with corbels in the form of angels occupied in minstrelsy. Above each of these angels — which were innovations — he placed, under richly crocketted canopies and standing on very finely-carved brackets, the figures of six saints. These were not innovations, though no signs of them appear in the engraving in Britton's "Cathedrals," where, indeed, the incomplete shafts just mentioned are to all appearance complete. But in Pennant's "Journey from Chester to London," 1782, the six statues are mentioned, and he tells us not only their names, but also that they were richly painted. The new statues represent the same original characters: St. Mary, St. Mary Magdalene, and St. Peter on the north side; St. James, St. Philip, and St. Christopher on the south: these with their niches have been executed partly from the old description of them and partly by reference to the niches remaining in the Lady Chapel.

An investigation of the roof proved that its bosses had been originally profusely gilded and painted, and that the ribs had been painted in tri-colour, though, oddly enough, this apparently had not been the case in the Lady Chapel. Mr Dyce, R.A., was called in to give an opinion, and suggested a large scheme, upon which he actually started, but after having proceeded only a small way, difficulties arose and he departed. What little paint had been applied to the ribs was removed; but a few of the more easterly bosses remain gilt to this day, and afterwards the others were reddened to bring out the sculpture.

The architectural history of the choir and presbytery is very interesting. There is practically no documentary evidence at all to tell when and how it was built; and what we know about it now is due to the antiquarian skill of the late Professor Willis. Nothing can have been more fortunate than that he should have been able to make an inspection of the foundations of the choir, for no man had a greater genius for using the smallest discoveries to the greatest advantage. Numerous stories are told of his extraordinary gift for divining what was to be found. As Canon Lonsdale says: "He knew, as it were, by instinct

THE CHOIR IN 1820.

what was hidden under the soil. 'Dig there,' he said, and the base he wanted came to light. 'Open out the earth here,' and the solid piece of stone which he had been looking for to complete his imaginary plan was straightway disclosed to view." He came here in August 1859, when excavations were being made in the choir, and on what he saw then he based the theory of the growth of the cathedral which has found favour with everyone ever since. The nature of his discoveries here, and the conclusions he drew from them, have been briefly given in the section of this book devoted to the history of the cathedral, so that it is unnecessary to further discuss them, except when they apply to buildings which are now in existence.

The present choir was commenced at the very beginning of the thirteenth century. Of this choir only the lower portions of the three bays nearest the tower remain above ground, but there is no doubt that the original eastern termination had been removed to make way for the beautiful presbytery which now remains and extends eastward, with its vaulting at the same elevation as that of the choir. This was done probably immediately after the Lady Chapel had been built, or at the same time, and it is supposed that the work proceeded from the east end and the old choir was gradually pulled down, leaving the three western bays standing, and that then the clerestory of these bays was replaced by work in uniformity with that in the new presbytery; at the same time the front half of their pier arches was removed and mouldings given to them corresponding to those in the presbytery, their piers were also slightly altered. In this way the choir and presbytery acquired a uniform appearance, both inside and out; for the portion of the old side aisle on the south is hidden by the sacristy, and that on the north by the chapter-house and vestibule.

As has been said, only one of the original Decorated clerestory windows now remain; the others, it may be supposed, were destroyed in the sieges of the Civil War, for they have been replaced with Perpendicular tracery which belongs to a period when this style was only being imitated; it was probably put in at the Restoration.

The high altar is now placed between the sixth pair of piers (counting from the west). This is probably the old arrangement, but until the recent restorations the altar was placed in the Lady Chapel: the pier arches of the choir were walled up, and a large screen placed in the eastern tower arch; so that the choir and Lady Chapel were converted into one long aisleless chapel.

Photochrom Co. Ltd., Photo.]
THE CHOIR, LOOKING EAST.

It is very interesting to note the signs in the choir of the attempt to combine the two styles which, as has been explained, met here. The third piers stand on the line of demarcation between the part retained and the part rebuilt, and consequently carry an Early English arch to the west and a Decorated arch to the east. The Early English column was partially cut away and partially used in the new work, as may be seen on inspection of these piers. It will also be seen that the vaulting in the aisles is much rougher in the old part than in the eastern bays. The plaster used to hide this; but Sir Gilbert Scott caused it to be removed, and is said afterward to have regretted having done so.

Another interesting junction between two buildings of

Photochrom Co. Ltd., Photo.]

SOUTH AISLE OF CHOIR, LOOKING EAST.

different dates is the entrance to the vestibule of the chapter-house. This entrance is in the third bay of the north aisle, and is obviously a combination of doorway and window, as may be seen by comparing the window of the first bay with it.

Again, in the first bays of the aisles there are windows in the Early English style, but they look only into the aisles of the transepts; showing, as has before been stated, that the transept aisles were not originally contemplated, and certainly did not take the place of earlier Norman aisles.

The arch at the west end of the north choir aisle is

THE CHOIR, LOOKING WEST.

F

decorated with a double chevron moulding—evidence that it is one of the oldest pieces of work left in the cathedral. This arch has at a more recent date been lined with another arch of the Decorated period, probably in order to strengthen it.

The arcading in the aisles is very interesting. In the first three western bays in both aisles the large arcading, with its plain trefoiled arches, is clearly Early English. The arcading in the other bays is equally clearly of the Decorated period, and is considerably smaller. In the four eastern bays in each aisle the arches go right up to the course which forms the top of the arcading, and the triangular spandrels thus formed are ornamented each with a curious little head, having queer headgear; the rest of the spandrel is carved with foliage, and in the plates of the foliated arches are quaint animals. The arcading in the remaining bay is similar, but angels' heads with wings take up the whole spandrel. Some of the arcading, notably that in the three easterly bays of the south aisle, is unrestored. The inferiority of the modern work in the next bay is only too patent.

In the south choir aisle the third window from the east has very beautiful carved work, the splays being covered with two bands of richly-carved foliage. Under the window is now the tomb of Bishop Hacket, and Dean Heywood's monument is said to have also been in this place.

In the south aisle, over the entrance to the sacristy, there is a very charmingly-proportioned gallery which is known as the "minstrel gallery." A gallery of this kind, though not unique, is very rare, but Exeter Cathedral has two—one in the north transept and another in the nave. In this case the arcading has been altered to accommodate this obviously later addition, made probably in the early part of the fifteenth century. Three shafts from the arcade have been left, which support a fan-shaped vaulting, upon which the gallery rests. There is little doubt as to the object of the gallery, though various theories have been advanced. By some it is supposed that it was used by the priest whose duty it was to watch the lights burning on the various altars; others suggest that it was indeed used by the instrumentalists to keep time during the procession, etc.; but, as it is immediately in front of the chapel of the Head of St. Chad, it was no doubt intended for the exhibition of the head to those below

in the aisle.   However, it may be said that the raised
galleries in mediæval halls were always called by the name
of "minstrel gallery," and so the name came to be used of
galleries generally.   This gallery is reached by the staircase
in the wall which leads to the upper floor of the sacristy.
Just against the entrance to this staircase, in the wall of
the aisle, is an ancient piscina.   Its presence here is unex-
plained, as there is no record of a chapel at this spot ;
though it has been suggested that the altar dedicated to
St. Blaise occupied a position in this aisle.

It is perhaps worth noticing that in the old days the two
bays of the cathedral between the high altar and the Lady
Chapel, together with their portions of the aisles, were generally spoken of as the Lady Choir, and are marked as such in
old plans ; other writers again speak of this part of the building as "the cross aisle."   There were gates across the choir
aisles in a line with the reredos, and these are marked in the
plan of the cathedral published somewhere about 1720.   No
doubt the eastern ends of the choir aisles in still earlier days
were spoken of as St. Andrew's Chapel or St. Nicholas' Chapel ;
but, though it is almost certain that the east end of the north
choir aisle was dedicated to St. Andrew, there is no certain information as to the dedication of the corresponding chapel in
the south aisle, but it is generally believed to have contained
an altar to St. Nicholas.

The Choir Screen was designed by Sir Gilbert Scott and
Mr J. B. Phillips, and executed by Mr Skidmore of Coventry.
It is a very highly-ornamented structure in wrought-iron,
copper, and brass, and is said to have been the first screen of
this kind ; but other screens of the same character are now to
be seen at Salisbury, Worcester, Hereford, and other churches.
The capitals are of hammered copper ; there are imitations of
various fruits in ivory, onyx, and red and white cornelian : on
the upper part, on each side, are eight angels with instruments
of music ; the whole is surmounted with a frieze of open scroll
work, and a cross rises from the top of the pedimented gateway in the centre.   The side iron gates into the choir aisles
were also executed by Mr Skidmore.

The Stalls are modern, and are somewhat disappointing.
The canons' stalls have no canopies, and their absence certainly deprives the choir of a feature generally to be found in

S. B. Bolas & Co., Photo.]

UNDER THE CENTRAL TOWER.

cathedrals.   Otherwise, the stalls are a satisfactory instance of
modern carving, and were carried out by Mr Evans of Ella-
stone in Derbyshire.   He is always said to have been the
original of Seth in " Adam Bede," and he certainly was a cousin
of the great authoress.   There is much natural foliage in the
carving, with figures of apostles, kings, and bishops, and
panels representing scenes from Old Testament history.   The
Bishop's Throne is by the same artist.

The Reredos is a very gorgeous piece of work, but it must
be confessed that the effect is again not wholly satisfactory.
It might even be said that in the endeavour to attain magnificence, over-elaboration has ended in a tawdry appearance.
However, tastes differ, and this reredos has its admirers.   It
was designed by Sir Gilbert Scott, and cost £2000, which
sum was raised by the Honourable Mrs H. Howard, the wife
of the dean.   It was part of the scheme that all the materials
for the reredos should come from the diocese, and with the
exception of the green malachite, this idea has been carried
out.   The alabaster came from near Tutbury, and the marbles
from Derbyshire (then in the diocese): and the Duke of Devon-
shire was induced to give some of the beautiful red marble,
which bears the name of the " Duke's red," from his quarry, so
rarely opened.

In the centre is a bas-relief of the Ascension, with a figure
of " The Lamb " underneath ; on each side are two compartments containing the emblems of the four evangelists.
All five compartments are surmounted with very highly-
decorated pediments, the central one being the largest and
most magnificent ; above it rises a very elaborate pinnacle,
ending in a cross.   There is an open arcading on each side,
extending to the piers of the presbytery.   The pediments
have each a head in the centre, and between the pediments
are angels with ivory trumpets.

The reredos has purposely been kept very low, so that the
view of the glass in the Lady Chapel may be intercepted as little
as possible.   One cannot help feeling that too much was sacri-
ficed to that idea.   One of the main principles of the Gothic
builder, it has been said, was to suggest an air of mystery.
The light screen and the low reredos have the very opposite
effect ; and it may be prophesied that the days of their admiration are rapidly coming to an end.

The Sedilia are interesting on account of the canopies, which are old, and probably formed part of the original high altar screen.   Their style is that known as Perpendicular, but they obviously belong to its early period.   No doubt the screen suffered grievously after the siege ; and at the Restoration of the monarchy and the cathedral a wooden screen was erected in front of it.   Pennant, who saw it in 1780, says : " The beauty of the choir was much impaired by the impropriety of a rich altar-piece, of Grecian architecture, terminating this elegant Gothic building."

This arrangement came to an end in 1788, when Wyatt threw the choir and Lady Chapel into one long chapel, and the old altar screen was utilised in the choir screen and helped to support the organ.   When this screen in turn was taken down, the old canopies, much battered and largely repaired with plaster, were examined, and found to be of Bath stone, and in this the repairs were executed.   Six of them were used for the sedilia, and the other three are to be found just behind, over the effigy of Dean Howard.

The Pavement between the stalls is of tiles, made after the pattern of old tiles which were found in the cathedral.   The modern ones are by Messrs Minton.   There is some record of how the cathedral has at various times been paved, as Dr Plot tells us that " the old floor of the choir was paved lozengy with cannel coal and alabaster, the former got at Beaudesert," and at one time the nave and aisles were paved with brick.   Some of the old tiles and two slabs of coal are preserved in the floor of the consistory court.

The pavement in the presbytery is different, and is made principally of incised stone, with marble borders.   There are four large medallions, which show scenes in the history of the diocese, and these are surrounded with representations of kings and bishops who have had some connection with the see.   The general scheme was arranged by Sir Gilbert Scott, but the medallions were designed by the Rev. J. Pitman, headmaster of Rugeley Grammar School.   The first medallion represents the consecration of St. Chad as Bishop of York ; round it are Oswy, King of Northumbria and Mercia, who was the principal instrument in introducing Christianity into Mercia ; Diuma, first Bishop ; Wulphere, King of Mercia ; and Jaruman, Bishop of Mercia, the immediate predecessor of St. Chad.

S. B. Bolas & Co., Photo.]

THE REREDOS.

The second medallion gives the well-known story of Theodore, the great archbishop, setting St. Chad on a horse; around are Ethelred, king of Mercia after Wulphere; Sexwulf, the bishop who divided up the diocese; Offa, King of Mercia, who made Lichfield an archbishopric, and Higbert, the archbishop.

The third medallion shows the translation of St. Chad's bones from Stowe Church, where they were buried, to the cathedral; around are Stephen, who was king when Bishop Roger de Clinton built the Norman cathedral; Henry III., who gave stone for the transept; and Bishop Langton, who built the Lady Chapel.

The fourth medallion shows the procession to the chapter-house for divine service at the Restoration (1660); around are Charles II. and Bishop Hacket, who then restored the cathedral; Queen Victoria and Bishop Lonsdale, who was bishop at the time of the recent restorations.

The altar space is covered with encaustic tiles, given by Mr C. Minton Campbell. In the centre is the Feast of the Passover, and around are shown Cain and Abel, Melchisedec blessing Abraham, Abraham and Isaac, Joseph and his brethren, Moses striking the Rock, and the Brazen Serpent—all Old Testament types of the Divine Sacrifice.

The Monuments in the south choir aisle are particularly interesting. Commencing from the west end, there is on the south side an altar tomb in memory of Archdeacon Hodson, who died in 1855. The slab is of Serpentine stone, with a brass cross inlaid, and there are alabaster plaques representing the Crucifixion, the Entombment, the Resurrection, and the Ascension. Opposite is a monument to his son, Major Hodson, known as "Hodson of Hodson's Horse," who played a dramatic part in the Indian Mutiny, where he received his death wound. The coped top forms a cross, and underneath are represented the King of Delhi surrendering his sword to Major Hodson, with allegorical figures of Justice, Fortitude, Temperance, and Mercy; and at the corners statuettes of Joshua, David, St. Thomas of India, and St. George of England. Both these monuments are by Mr G. E. Street, R.A., the well-known architect of the Law Courts in London.

Close to the gate is a medallion to Erasmus Darwin, "a skilful observer of Nature," and the author of several books. He died in 1802, and was the grandfather of Charles Darwin, the celebrated biologist, whose name is a household word. The memorial to the grandfather directs attention to the hereditary obligations of the grandson.

In the second bay, between the pier arches, is the monument of Bishop Langton, who died in 1296. This originally stood to the south of the high altar. The figure is of Purbeck marble, and is habited *in pontificalibus*; the head lies on a plain cushion in a kind of frame. The mitre and shoes were probably once richly jewelled, and the whole, as we know from Sir William Dugdale's " Visitation," had a pedimented canopy. Now nothing remains but the mutilated effigy.

In a similar position in the third bay is the effigy of Bishop Patteshull, who died in 1241. This is also of Purbeck marble, and was probably jewelled. There are ministering angels outside a pediment at the head ; the figure has the pastoral staff in the left hand, while the right is obviously raised in benediction, though only the fingers are left, the second wearing the episcopal ring. Pennant and others have drawn attention to the fact that this effigy has the " stigmata " or marks of Our Lord's wounds on his hands and feet. Some antiquarians think that this is the monument of Bishop Weseham, and not of Bishop Patteshull. There are engravings and descriptions of these last two monuments in Gough's "Sepulchral Monuments in Great Britain," 1796, but it is certainly strange that Langton's monument is described as Patteshull's, and *vice versa*.

Opposite to Bishop Langton is the most curious monument in the cathedral. It has now been identified as the tomb of Sir John Stanley of Pipe. The effigy represents a knight naked to the waist, below which was formerly a deep skirt painted with the arms of Stanley, the legs being in armour, while under the head is a buck's horn, and a similar horn is placed beneath the feet. The whole subject of this tomb is one presenting many difficulties, but they have now been cleared up, and in a communication to the "Archæological Journal," vol. 24, Mr J. Hewitt has given much interesting information. From it the following account is taken :— The monument was always known as that of "Captain Stanley," who for some offence had been excommunicated, and who, after atonement, had been admitted to sepulture in holy ground on condition that the evidence of his punishment should appear on his sepultured effigy. The mutilations

of the Civil Wars have so defaced the monument as to make
this story extremely doubtful, until among papers belonging
to the Earl of Winchelsea was found a coloured drawing
of this effigy, done by Sir William Dugdale just before the
wars for Sir Christopher Hatton. This sketch showed that
the skin was bare, and that the skirt had the Stanley arms.
But this did not clear up the difficulty. Pennant, in his
" Journey from Chester to London," describes the tomb
and gives the story, and then says : " I find a Sir Humphrey
Stanley of Pipe, who died in the reign of Henry VII., who
had a squabble with the Chapter about conveying water
through his lands to the close . . . so probably this
might be the gentleman who incurred the censure of the
church for his impiety." Shaw, in his " History of Staffordshire," declares that the arms on the base of the tomb show
"the arms of Stanley impaling or, three chevronels gules
(Clare)," which means that the person represented married
a Clare. This Sir Humphrey did not do, and, moreover,
he was buried in Westminster Abbey, where his brass still
remains. Further investigation showed that the arms of
Clare are also the arms of Gerard, and then that Sir John
Stanley of Pipe married Margaret, the daughter of Sir Thomas
Gerard. Pipe is a domain about a mile from Lichfield, so
that the family of the dead knight would naturally have
desired his interment in the cathedral of that city.

It does not appear that there was any ignominy implied
in scourging as a public penance. On the contrary, many
royal personages have submitted to it, and everyone will
remember that Henry II. underwent a scourging upon his
naked shoulders by the hands of the monks of Canterbury.
There is a stained-glass window in the Bodleian Library
at Oxford showing this scene.

Dr Rock, in the same volume of the " Archæological
Journal," says that to his thinking "this Stanley, of knightly
rank, had drawn upon himself the greater excommunication
through the spilling of blood in Lichfield Cathedral on some
occasion, from a blow on the face with his hand or possibly
by a slight stab with his avelace on the person of one with
whom he had quarrelled. He lies bareheaded and naked
as far down as the girdle. His upraised hands, according
to the representation given by Pennant, and copied in Shaw's

' History of Staffordshire,' held a scroll which must have been
the document . . . signifying under the bishop's hand
that, having undergone the canonical penance, the offender
was again admitted to all Christian privileges."

Farther east than the "minstrel gallery" there is a window
in memory of Bishop Rawle, who was consecrated Bishop
of Trinidad in this cathedral by Bishop Selwyn. The subjects
depicted in the window are Christ's Appeal to St. Peter,
St. Paul's Vision, and The Baptism of the Ethiopian by
St. Philip. Underneath the window is a highly-ornamented
altar tomb designed by Sir Gilbert Scott in memory of
Archdeacon Moore, whose effigy lies on the top. He died
in 1876. Opposite, in the next bay, is the monument of
Dean Howard, who died in 1868 ; the effigy of the dean, in
marble, lies under a triple canopy formed from portions of
the old screen. These last two effigies were the work of
H. Armstead, R.A. It was here that Bishop Langton's
monument once stood, and here also was Bishop Hacket's.
This last now stands on the opposite side under the very
beautiful window of the sixth bay of this aisle : it is in the
Jacobean style, and is much painted and gilded. An effigy
of the Bishop lies on an altar tomb under a canopy, while
in front is a lengthy inscription in Latin.

Near this place, with other monuments, is one to the
memory of Colonel Richard Bagot, who received his death
wound at the battle of Naseby, 1645, and was buried in the
cathedral. His father was Sir Hervey Bagot, Governor of
the Close on behalf of the king.

In the seventh bay is another of the semi-effigies, two of
which are in the south aisle of the nave, but this one is much
more damaged ; it is supposed to be the monument of Canon
Strangeways. In Jackson's "History of Lichfield," which was
published in 1805, it is stated that the name, though not then
distinguishable, had only recently become obliterated, and was
known and remembered to be Strangeways.

On the south wall, towards the east are, amongst others,
brasses to Dean Champneys, 1875, and Dean Bickersteth,
1892, and above these there is a monument to Canon Horton,
who died in 1728.

Two windows have recently been ornamented with new glass
by Mr Kempe, showing scenes taken from the Acts of the

Apostles; one, in memory of Dr H. W. Hewitt, represents Peter and Paul healing the lame man at the Beautiful Gate of the temple. The other is in memory of Mr J. T. Godfrey Faussett, and represents Stephen before the Council, having delivered his apology, looking up and declaring "Behold I see the heavens opened, and the Son of Man standing on the right hand of God."

At the east end of this aisle, on the spot where probably once stood the altar of St. Nicholas, is the famous monument

Photochrom Co. Ltd., Photo.]
THE SLEEPING CHILDREN.

known as "The Sleeping Children." This was executed by Sir Francis Chantrey, R.A., and set up in 1817. It is said that this monument established his fame. Britton, in 1820, devotes more than two large quarto pages—a great space for him—to ecstasies over it, and no doubt the taste of the time demanded undiluted admiration. Now we may prize it as an early example of the new style which, in art as well as in literature, was to supersede the artifice of the eighteenth century: the essence of that new style was, Mr Walter Pater tells us, "an intimate consciousness of the expression of natural things."

The monument is in memory of the two daughters of the Reverend William Robinson, Prebendary of the cathedral, and represents the young children locked in each other's arms.

Behind it is a wall memorial to their father, and to the side is a piscina, which has at the back of it an old fresco, probably of the fourteenth century. The subject is the Crucifixion, with figures of St. Mary and St. John, one on each side of our Lord. The illustration is from a drawing preserved in the National Art Library, South Kensington Museum. The window at the end of the aisle contains some of the old Flemish glass, which has in the centre a curious representation of the Trinity.

In leaving this aisle it may be noted that tradition has it that between the pillars of the eighth bay was the monument of Lord Basset: that the tomb of Bishop William de Corkhull was between the pillars of the seventh bay, and that, in a similar position in the fifth bay, was buried Bishop de Molend. The Ashmolean MSS. give a long description of Lord Basset's monument: " Between the choir and the chapel of the Blessed Mary is the monument of Ralph, Lord Basset. He is lying in complete armour, his hands erected, and thereon his gauntlets. On his head, which is laid upon his helm and crest, viz., a boar, is a steel cap, and on his right shoulder a square shield of his arms. His dagger is laid by his right side, and his feet are resting upon a boar." He died in the reign of Richard II. It is always said that Sir Walter Scott had this monument in his mind when he described Lord Marmion's monument :—

> " Fitz-Eustace care
> A pierced and mangled body bare
> To moated Lichfield's lofty pile ;
> And there, beneath the southern aisle,
> A tomb, with Gothic sculpture fair,
> Did long Lord Marmion's image bear,
> (Now vainly for its sight you look ;
> 'Twas levell'd when fanatic Brook
> The fair cathedral storm'd and took ;
> But thanks to Heaven and good St. Chad,
> A guerdon meet the spoiler had !)
> There erst was martial Marmion found,
> His feet upon a couchant hound,
> 　His hands to Heaven upraised ;
> And all around, on scutcheon rich
> And tablet carved, and fretted niche,
> 　His arms and feats were blazed."

F. G. M. Beaumont, Photo.]

FRESCO-PAINTING OF THE CRUCIFIXION IN THE SOUTH
CHOIR AISLE.

G

The accounts do not entirely tally, so that it may be the tomb described was as little Lord Basset's as it was really Lord Marmion's.

Not very far from this last tomb was the monument of William, Lord Paget, who was not buried here but at Drayton. He was ambassador from Henry VIII. to Charles V., and held other important posts under that king and his daughter, Queen Mary ; he died in 1563. There is an engraving of his monument in Shaw's "Staffordshire," which shows it to have been very magnificent.

The monuments in the **North Choir Aisle** are not only more scanty than those in other parts of the cathedral, but they are of less interest. At the east end is the kneeling figure of Bishop Ryder, who died in 1836. This monument is in white marble, and one of Chantrey's latest works, just as the more famous monument in a similar position in the south aisle is one of his earliest. It was originally intended that the figure should be on a higher pedestal, and no doubt the effect is not increased by its lower position.

Behind, on the east wall, is an inscription in memory of the bishop. The window above this contains some old Flemish glass, which has a figure of St. Christopher in the centre. The window in the north side in the corner is by Mr C. E. Kempe, in memory of Mr Patterson, late sub-chanter of the cathedral. The glass shows King David teaching the singers of the House of the Lord. Beneath is an ancient aumbry.

Opposite, between the pillars, is the traditional site of the burial-place of Bishop Stretton ; he is said to have been buried in St. Andrew's Chapel. There is little doubt that the end of this aisle contained an altar dedicated to that saint.

Between the next pair of pillars westward, it is said that Bishop Blythe was buried, but his monument at one time stood in the other aisle of the choir.

On the north side of the altar is the monument to the memory of Bishop Lonsdale, who died in 1867. The monument, which is highly decorative, consists of an effigy of the bishop lying on an altar-tomb of marble and alabaster. The effigy is by Mr G. F. Watts, R.A., the celebrated artist, and the tomb was designed by Sir Gilbert Scott, who is said to have taken the idea of the canopy, with its triple pediment, from the monument of John of Eltham in Westminster Abbey.

In the space between the next pair of pillars westward, Archbishop Scrope, formerly bishop of this diocese, is said to have been buried.   He was beheaded in 1405 by Henry IV.

In the most easterly bay but one of this aisle there must have been a doorway leading into the chapel which Dr Stukeley speaks of: "In the chapel over against the lady choir was the burying-place of two Mercian Kings; but it is now chosen for a burying-place by Dr Chandler, present bishop of Lichfield, who has there buried one child."

The Lady Chapel has always most justly been admired by architects and antiquarians.   Not only is it peculiarly beautiful in its construction, but also its windows are now filled with

BRACKETS IN THE LADY CHAPEL.

some of the most charming old glass to be seen in England. In shape it forms a symmetrical extension, both in height and width, to the choir, but without aisles; and it has an octagonal apse—the only example, it is said, of such a termination in the country.   It is lighted by nine high windows, with Decorated tracery.   This tracery has recently been restored in the style of that in the three end windows; until this was done most of the windows contained Perpendicular tracery.

The windows rest on an arcade of very beautiful design. The arcade may be said to consist of a series of small decorated canopies, supported by shafts with carved capitals, and separated by ornamented buttresses.   The canopies, which bow forward, have trefoil ogee arches, surmounted with crockets and finials.   Above the arcade is a similar embattled parapet to that in the choir, with a similar passage round the chapel behind it.

The vaulting of the roof is like that in the choir; the same number of ribs diverging from the slender shafts which run right down to the bends of the arcade.   Half-way up these shafts are niches, the brackets and canopies to which are beautifully carved. These are old, but until recently were empty, and no authentic record remained as to what were the characters represented. Dr Stukeley believed that the figures had been those of the five wise and five foolish virgins. This theory has not, however, found sufficient favour to lead to a reproduction of their effigies, for in 1895 the niches were filled with figures of ten virgin saints and martyrs. These were executed by Messrs Farmer & Brindley, from designs by Mr C. E. Kempe, and they may be warmly congratulated on their work. The statues are really beautiful, and are infinitely superior to most of the other modern sculpture in the cathedral. It will be noticed, too, that the figures seem the right size for the niches, instead of being much too large, as in many other cases. The statues are as follow :—

1. St. Werburga, with pastoral staff and book, and a model of Chester Cathedral at her feet.
2. St. Cecilia, with organ.
3. St. Prisca, with palm branch, and lion at her feet.
4. St. Faith, with sword and rack.
5. St. Catherine, with sword and wheel and open book, treading on a monster.
6. St. Margaret, with book and cross, treading on a dragon.
7. St. Lucy, with palm branch and lamp.
8. St. Agnes, with palm branch and book, and lamb at her feet.
9. St. Agatha, with palm branch and tongs.
10. St. Etheldreda, with crown and pilgrim staff, and pastoral staff and a model of Ely Cathedral at her feet.

The present altar-piece, which is in the form of a triptych, has scenes connected with the birth of Our Lord carved in relief. These are : The Annunciation, the Salutation of Elizabeth, the Nativity, the Presentation in the Temple, and the Adoration of the Magi. The doors, which can be closed, have paintings on the back representing David, Isaiah, St. John the Baptist, and St. Chad. There are four carved figures of St. Ambrose, St. Jerome, St. Augustine, and St. Gregory supporting the central panel. The altar rails are of alabaster. Before the recent alterations there was a plaster reredos, which had been placed there by Wyatt, and the continuity of the arcading and open carved work, which originally went right round the chapel, was thus broken. Sir Gilbert Scott is said to have been anxious not to remove the reredos, partly, perhaps, on account of the glass behind, which was known to be plain. However, the restoration to the original style has been made, and the plain glass replaced by a very excellent imitation of the Herkenrode glass, representing the three Marys. This was done by Messrs Burlison & Grylls with great skill. There was a screen between the Lady Chapel and the rest of the cathedral in old days. Stukeley mentions it in his notes. He says : " The partition there betwixt the two choirs is a fine piece of architecture, but demolished also in time of war ; and, though the figures are destroyed, and at the foot of the same every cherub defaced, yet it may be perceived to be a fine piece of work ; for though it be uniform from top to bottom, yet every capital and pedestall are different works within and without."

What is known of the building of the Lady Chapel has already been told in Chapter I. and in the account of the choir and presbytery. The founder of the chapel, Bishop Langton, was buried here, but his tomb was afterwards removed to the south side of the high altar. Shaw tells us of the monument at one time "in the east part of the chapel, towards the south," of Robert Master and Catherine, his wife, and says that " the drawing in Dugdale's ' Visitation ' represents them each under a round arch, in the attitude of prayer at a desk." No trace is left of this monument.

As might be expected from what has been given of the history of the cathedral, there is none of the old glass belonging to it remaining ; but in spite of this, all the nine windows of the Lady Chapel have very beautiful old glass in them. This glass is not Mediæval, but belongs to the sixteenth century, and the whole of it is a comparatively recent acquisition for the cathedral. That in the seven most eastern windows, and known as the Herkenrode glass, was put in at the beginning of the century ; and the other two windows which, until recently, held modern glass, bearing the arms of various dignitaries of the cathedral, have recently been enriched by old glass of probably very nearly the same period as the other.

The nine windows, for the purposes of explanation, may be numbered in succession 1 to 9. No. 1, being the first window

on the north, and No. 9, the first on the south, contain, therefore, the more recently acquired glass. This is supposed to
have come from the Low Countries; but, at anyrate, about
the middle of the century it was brought to England, and lay
for years in some cellars in London, where it was forgotten.
Finally, it was purchased from the representatives of the
Marquis of Ely. The glass shows the arms of the kingdom
of Aragon, and amongst other mottoes, that of Charles V.

No. 1. The lower compartment is a symbolic picture on the
subject of Baptism. Out of the waters in the fountain come
the children, to be received by their guardian spirits, while
above are figures representing Faith, Fortitude, and Love,
and still higher is a representation of the Divine Presence.
No. 9 is a pictorial representation of the legendary Death of
the Virgin Mary. The Virgin is represented lying in a
canopied bed, surrounded by the apostles, who have been
summoned to gather round her death-bed : they are all present
except St. Thomas, who has been detained at the baptism of a
royal prince. Above is a representation of the Virgin entering
into glory.

As stated above, these two windows had originally coats of
arms in them, and a reproduction of the arms appears in the
tracery of the windows, No. 1 having those of the dean and
chapter in 1803, and No. 9 those of the bishops of the diocese
from Bishop Hacket to that date.

The glass in the other seven windows — the Herkenrode
glass—was purchased in 1802 by Sir Brooke Boothby, who
discovered it in Belgium, where it had been hidden for
protection from the French. It had been taken from the
dissolved Abbey of Herkenrode, near Liege. There were
three hundred and forty pieces, each about twenty-two inches
square, and some of them are marked with dates between
1530 and 1540. Sir Brooke is said to have given two
hundred pounds for it ; but it has since been valued at fifteen
thousand pounds. He, however, most generously sold it
to the dean and chapter for the modest sum he had paid
for it. It turned out that there was enough to fill the seven
windows it now occupies in the Lady Chapel. Some portions
have been used in other windows of the cathedral, which
have been already described.

There is a considerable difference in appearance between

this glass and that in the other two windows. The subjects depicted in the latter are very distinct, while in the former they are more confused, and it must be said that the Herkenrode glass is much faded. Still, the whole of it is very beautiful, and if it does not satisfy those who crave after the Mediæval stained glass, it is certainly some of the finest glass of the kind to be found in England. The designs have been conjectured to be by Lambert Lombard, the first, and one of the most famous, of the Italianised Flemish School of the sixteenth century ; and the other glass belongs to the same period.

The abbey at Herkenrode was founded in 1182, and belonged to the Cistercian Order. It became noted for the

BRACKETS IN THE LADY CHAPEL.

miracles performed there ; from which reason, no doubt, it acquired great wealth, and increased so much in size that it was almost like a small town. All the nuns were of noble family. A history of the abbey was published in 1744, and a copy was presented to the cathedral library by Sir Brooke Boothby. The book contains a view of the abbey buildings, in the centre of which is seen the church. In the third window of the Lady Chapel is a similar picture of the church.

Windows Nos. 2 and 3 contain portraits of founders and benefactors of the abbey, with their patron saints. The other five windows, Nos. 4, 5, 6, and 7 show scenes in the life of Christ.

The following is a brief description of these windows :—

No. 2. In this window the glass is in four pictures. In the lower left-hand compartment is Cardinal Evrad de la Marck, Bishop of Liege, supported by St. Lambert ; and in the corresponding space to the right is Floris Egmont, Count de Buren, with his wife, attended by St. Christopher and St. Margaret. The picture above is of Maximilian Egmont,

Count de Buren, kneeling before an altar, and attended by St. Christopher and St. Barbara. The remaining picture on the left has John, Count de Horn, and his wife Anne, also kneeling before an altar. They are attended by St. John the Evangelist and St. Anne the mother of the Virgin.

No. 3 contains six pictures, which go right across the window—(1) the lowest, has the church of the abbey already mentioned, with an abbess and two nuns, and the Virgin and Child; (2) the Virgin and Child again, with an angel bearing a shield; (3) the Virgin and Child, an abbot and abbess of the Cistercian Order, and the Emperor Lotharius II.; (4) Agnes Mettecoven and her husband kneeling to St. Agnes, with her lamb; (5) St. John the Evangelist and St. Barbara, St. John the Baptist, and St. Margaret, with members of the Mettecoven family; (6) the highest, has Henry de Lechy and his wife, with St. Henry and St. Christina.

No. 4. Christ scourged, Christ crowned with thorns, the Annunciation.

No. 5, the central window. The Ascension, Christ and the two Disciples at Emmaus, the Three Marys (modern glass).

No. 6. The Last Supper, the Entry into Jerusalem, the Betrayal of Christ in the Garden of Gethsemane.

No. 7. The Day of Judgment, the Day of Pentecost, St. Thomas is reproved for his doubt.

No. 8. Pilate delivering Christ to be crucified, Christ bearing his Cross, the Descent from the Cross, the Resurrection.

On the south side of the Lady Chapel, between the buttresses, are three erections, which were no doubt built at the same time as the Lady Chapel itself. They have been known as "the Mortuary Chapels," and also as "the Vestries." They were probably built for the former purpose.

They have recently been restored as a memorial to Bishop Selwyn, who died in 1878. All three chapels have groined roofs, with ribs and bosses, and in the floor some of the old encaustic tiles still remain. The central chapel is the largest, and is lighted by two small windows. It is only entered from the eastern chapel by means of a doorway cut right through the buttress. In this central chapel lies the effigy, in Derbyshire alabaster, of Bishop Selwyn. During his life he had expressed a wish to be buried here, but this was

found to be illegal, and he was buried in the close just outside. The effigy is by Mr Nicholls, and the decorations of
the walls of the chapel are by Messrs Clayton & Bell.
These show the arms of the bishopric of New Zealand, to
which the bishop was originally consecrated, and the arms
of the dioceses formed out of it, and there are more than
usually hideous frescoes showing the labours of the bishop
among the Maories and among the pitmen of the English
diocese. Here he is not likely to be forgotten ; and at
Cambridge there is a college known as Selwyn College,
founded with a similar idea to that which at Oxford caused
Keble College to be erected to the memory of another great
modern churchman : there also his memory will remain.

The western chapel has, at its north-western corner, a stair-
way leading to three cryptal chambers whose flooring is the
solid rock.

The Sacristy.—The building on the south side of the choir,
which is generally known as the " sacristy," is a very interesting part of the cathedral. Professor Willis decided that it
was erected at the same time as the original Early English
choir, and no doubt it belongs to the same period. A careful
inspection, however, especially of the entrance from the
" minstrel gallery " to the chapel of St. Chad's Head, which
now forms the top storey, shows unmistakable signs that,
like the entrance to the vestibule in the corresponding bay
of the north choir aisle, this doorway was once a window,
similar, no doubt, to those two still remaining—one in each
aisle — which look into the aisles of the transepts. This
being so, it is obvious that the " sacristy," or, at anyrate, the
upper storey, was an afterthought, and that it is later, though
perhaps only a little, than the choir, its date corresponding
perhaps with that of the south transept.

The upper storey, which until recently was used as the
muniment room, was originally the chapel of St. Chad's Head.
It has now been restored as a chapel through the zeal and
munificence of the present dean, Dr Luckock, and was
re-dedicated and re-opened on St. Chad's Day, March 2nd of
this year, 1897. In the order of service of that day the dean
gave an account of the chapel as follows :—

" The Chapel of St. Chad, first Bishop of Lichfield, and,
with the Blessed Virgin Mary, patron of our Cathedral Church,

was destroyed in all probability when the rest of the Cathedral
was laid in ruins in 1643, the siege beginning on St. Chad's
Day, March 2nd of that year. Little was left: the four walls
remained in a broken condition, with the vaulting-shafts and
caps for the springers of the stone groining, and the wall-ribs,
to mark its original lines; also the very beautiful Early
English windows—twelve lancets in groups of three—which,
singularly enough, were little injured. Externally these are
very plain, but internally they are full of interest, and there is
nothing better of the kind in the Cathedral. The site of the
old altar is clearly marked; indeed, a small portion of it has
been preserved. The piscina also still remains. After the
destruction the chapel must have been left roofless for years,
as, on breaking up the floor which had been raised by some
accumulation of rubbish, the workmen found roots of shrubs
embedded in it. At some time quite unknown, the chapel
was roofed in again, and the tops of the walls rebuilt where
they had been broken down. A flat plaster ceiling was
inserted, and being divided into two rooms, the old chapel
was filled with cupboards and used till last year for the custody
of the muniments. The aumbry remains in which antiquarians
suppose that St. Chad's relics were preserved. Dr Cox, in his
Catalogue of the muniments, page 90, throws some light upon
the subject, from the Chapter Act Books, quoting from F. 4
in the year 1481 :—'Two monstrances given to the Cathedral
in charge of William Hukyns, the custodian of the Head of
St. Chad by Dean Heywood, for keeping relics.' And he
appends the following note :—'This very likely gives the date
of the stone gallery in front of the muniment room in the
South Choir aisle (then the chapel of the head of St. Chad).
This gallery is of Perpendicular work, and was chiefly intended
for the exhibition of relics, in monstrances, to the pilgrims in
the aisle below; the second staircase, that allowed of a flow of
pilgrims to the upper chapel, being at this time removed.' All
the stone groining and the wood and iron work have been
completely restored under the direction of Mr J. Oldrid Scott.
There are some very old pieces of stone figure-work, which
have been preserved. The new bosses and corbels have been
carved with subjects from the history of St. Chad, the chief of
which show his being mounted on horseback, by Archbishop
Theodore; his protection of the hart that fled to him for

refuge; and his death in his cell, surrounded by angels. The reredos, of Staffordshire alabaster, replacing one the existence of which at the east end is clearly indicated, is of a very uncommon design, by Mr C. E. Kempe. It consists of an altar-piece of ornamental arcading, surmounted by three tall canopied niches in which are placed sculptured figures representing the Crucifixion, St. Mary, and St. John. These are supported by angels bearing shields. All the windows are filled with stained glass by Mr Kempe, and contain Choirs of Angels singing the Confessor's hymn, or Psalm cxii., *Beatus vir*, which runs in scrolls through nine of the lights. The angels over the crucifix in the east window bear a scroll with the words of Psalm xxi. 3, *Posimisti in capite*, etc. St. Chad is represented in the centre lancet of the west wall."

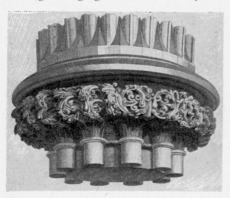

CAPITAL IN CHAPTER-HOUSE.

This chapel is now approached by a staircase, leading from a doorway in the fourth bay on to the gallery, usually and incorrectly known as the "minstrel gallery," from which again two short flights of steps, right and left, lead into the chapel.

The lower storey was originally the sacristy; it is now used as the consistory court. Against the west wall are some of the old Jacobean stalls, which were put into the choir in Bishop Hacket's time; while in the corner are let into the floor some of the old tiles and slabs of cannel coal with which, and alabaster, the cathedral was at one time paved. The windows are filled with Perpendicular tracery, replacing the old Early English windows. Underneath, and reached by a staircase in the southeast turret, now closed, is a vault, at present used as the burial vault of the Paget family. Probably it was once a dungeon.

In the west wall can be seen the place where a doorway led
into a chamber built in between the sacristy and the south
transept aisle. This was no doubt the treasury of the cathedral,
where all the most precious relics and valuables were kept. It
is now entered by a doorway in the choir aisle. At present it
appears to be a receptacle for odds and ends, and cupboards
are placed along the walls. On the west side are several large
aumbries, in which, no doubt, the relics were kept. The floor

Photochrom Co. Ltd., Photo.]

THE CHAPTER-HOUSE.

in this chamber has been raised at some time or other, and it
is now much higher than that of the adjoining consistory court,
so that there are steps in the south-east corner leading to a
door into the consistory court. This is not the old doorway
already mentioned, which is blocked up, but probably a much
later entrance. Some old cannon balls which have been discovered in and round the cathedral may be seen in the treasury.
On the north wall in both the consistory court and the treasury
can be seen the remains of an old course or housing which,
though in both cases incomplete, appears to have a semi-circular
form. No theory seems to have been advanced as to these
remains, and in this book it were wiser to follow precedent.

The Chapter-House, which lies to the north of the choir, is approached by a vestibule which has a doorway, already described, into the third bay of the north choir aisle. Both the chapter-house and the vestibule were built at the same time as the north transept—that is, somewhere near the middle of the thirteenth century—and the style is therefore that known as the Early English, but it is a later instance than that part of the choir into which the doorway leads. That the vestibule was not built when the early part of the choir was finished is evident, as "its walls abut against those of the choir with a straight joint, and the arch of entrance in the side aisle is a manifest intrusion into the space once occupied by a window." The north end of the vestibule has also been altered, there having been a doorway where now there is a window; the former existed until nearly the end of the last century, but it had been altered before the plate in Britton's "Cathedrals" was engraved. It can easily be seen from the outside that such a door must have existed, from the different colouring of the stone-work. The window has recently been filled with stained glass by Messrs Burlison & Grylls, representing Nehemiah and Simeon, in memory of the late verger, William Yeend. Down each side of the vestibule there is a very fine arcading, that on the west side being double and much deeper than that on the east, which is single; the niches are large enough to be used as seats, and it has been suggested that here the ceremony of washing the feet of the poor took place on Maundy Thursday; as there were thirteen niches, this is highly probable. Some of the capitals of the pillars of the arcade are very finely carved, and, as was usual at the time, are very deeply under-cut; and the dripstones terminate in very interesting corbels in the form of heads and bunches of foliage. Recently, on the west side, some of the arcading has been opened out to afford access to the new vestry, which has been constructed by roofing in the space between the vestibule and the north transept. On the east side near the cathedral is the entrance to the library, which is the upper storey of the chapter-house building, and is approached by a spiral staircase. At the farther end, on the same side, is the very fine entrance to the chapter-house. This, like the central west doorway and that in the north transept, is double and recessed. The mouldings in the arch are deeply and finely cut, and the capitals of the grouped shafts are very

richly carved with delicate leaves. The jambs have an enrich-
ment of dog-toothing behind the slender detached shafts, and
the two small arches have trefoil archivolts, so that the whole
has a very rich effect. In the tympanum of the arch there is a
bas-relief figure of Our Lord in a quatrefoil recess.

The chapter-house is a very fine room ; it is octagonal in
shape, but the north and south sides of it are double the length
of each of the other six sides, which are equal. There is a

EASTERN PORTION OF THE ARCADE IN THE CHAPTER-HOUSE.

central pillar, the clustered shafts of which are banded in the
centre ; the capitals of these shafts have a particularly rich and
elaborate carving of foliage ; and above, the vaulting ribs spread
to the roof like the branches of a tree, producing a very fine
effect. The bosses where the ribs intersect are also worthy of
attention, and the ribs rise from very richly-carved and deeply-
moulded corbels. The windows are Early English, and of two
lights each. Below is a very beautiful arcading, similar, indeed,
to that in the vestibule, which entirely surrounds the building.
The arcade is composed of deep, moulded, trefoil arches,

resting on single columns, with beautifully-carved capitals, in some of which will be found figures of birds and animals. The canopies of the arches are dog-toothed, and end in curiously-carved heads, which afford interesting illustrations of the head-dresses of the time.

The chapter-house was decorated with frescoes and stained glass by Dean Heywood in the fifteenth century, as we know from the MSS. entitled *Cantaria Sancti Blasii* in the library. The frescoes have disappeared except over the doorway, where still remain faint signs of the representation of the Assumption, which may have formed part of Dean Heywood's decoration, but more likely is earlier : it has been suggested that it was placed there by Bishop Burghill from the fact that a Dominican Friar, to which order he belonged, is represented in the group in adoration. The glass contained figures of the apostles, with other pictures above ; these being all pre-Cromwellian, have, of course, disappeared. More recently the glazing of the chapter-house displayed armorial bearings, more or less correct, in imitation of glass known to have ornamented the cathedral in the past. This armorial glass is gradually giving way to glass representing scenes in the history of the cathedral. At present, five of the windows have been so glazed, and the rest will be changed gradually, as opportunity offers.

The first window on the left-hand side on entering is in memory of Prebendary Edwards. There are figures of St. Chad and King Wulphere, with scenes showing the Consecration of St. Chad, and the Baptism by St. Chad of the two sons of King Wulphere.

The second window is in memory of Archdeacon Allen and Prebendary de Bunsen. The figures are St. Oswald and St. Aidan. The scenes represent St. Aidan preaching to the Northumbrians, with King Oswald interpreting ; and St. Aidan at Lindisfarne, teaching in his school, where St. Chad is one of the scholars.

The third window is in memory of Dean Bickersteth. The figures are Archbishop Theodore and St. Ovin, and the scenes St. Chad teaching his clergy, and St. Ovin listening to the angels who were calling St. Chad at his death.

The fourth window is in memory of Prebendary Gresley. The figures are Oswy, King of Northumbria, and Diuma, the first bishop of Mercia. The scenes are Bishop Jaruman promising to build a church at Lichfield, and the institution by King Æthelwald of prebendaries.

The fifth window is in memory of Prebendary Finch Smith. The figures represent Archbishop Higbert of Lichfield, and Thomas Cantelupe, Bishop of Hereford, formerly prebendary of this cathedral. The scenes are Bishop Aldulf at the Council of Cloveshoo, renouncing the metropolitan powers in favour of Canterbury, and Bishop Roger de Clinton building a new cathedral in honour of St. Mary and St. Chad.

The Library is immediately above the chapter-house, and is of the same octagonal shape. The arrangements also are similar, but the room is less lofty, the carvings less elaborate, and there is no arcading. Otherwise, we find the same central pillar, from which similar vaulting ribs spring, with corbels in the walls to receive them. It is not known for what purpose this room was originally intended, but certainly, until recent years, it was not used as a library. The old library, of which there are pictures by Hollar and King, stood to the north of the north transept in the close, or, as it is recorded in the Capitular Acts, vol. 3, "ex parte boreali in cimeterio." Dean Heywood gave £40 to build the library, and though it was not begun in his time, it was completed in the time of his successor, Dean Yotton, who also subscribed to its erection. This was at about the commencement of the sixteenth century, and the building remained until the middle of the eighteenth, when it was demolished.

The extent of the library has been increased by opening a doorway into the room above the vestibule. This room, it has recently been decided, was the old chapel of St. Peter. Though an upstairs chapel was not usual, yet it is not by any means unknown, and chapels were even sometimes to be found in the rood lofts of cathedrals. No trace can be found of the fresco, mentioned by Stukeley, of "St. Peter crucified with his head downwards, and two other apostles, etc." He tells us that the chapel was in his time used as a place for storing scaffolding and ladders, and that here was placed the mutilated remains of St. Chad's tomb.

The place still shows signs of its ill-usage, little having been done to repair the ravages of the Civil War. The vaulting is much broken, and the walls cracked : these facts strengthen the belief in the tradition that it was on this building, together with the choir, that the great central tower fell during the siege by the soldiers of the Parliament.

The library has had many generous donations of books at various times. Under the will of Frances, Duchess of Somerset, the cathedral received the library of her late husband, the Duke, who succeeded his grandfather as Earl of Hertford, and was restored to the family dukedom at the Restoration. The duchess was the daughter of the Earl of Essex who was the favourite of Queen Elizabeth, and whom she afterwards had beheaded. These books numbered about one thousand, and included many rare old Black-Letter chronicles and histories printed in the sixteenth and seventeenth centuries.

Many others have contributed to the library, amongst whom are Archdeacon Davies, 1763; William Smallbroke, 1771; Canon Lamb, 1770; Richard Hurd, 1777; Bishop Cornwallis, 1783; Rev. Henry White, 1786; Dr Pegge, the well-known antiquary, who, amongst other things, wrote an account of the life of Bishop Weseham, and who left the library, by his will, one hundred books out of his own library; Andrew Newton, who left his books to the cathedral, and built the college in the close for the widows and orphans of the clergy, besides spending large sums on educational purposes; and Sir Brooke Boothby, 1815, who gave the "History of the Abbey of Herckenrode," referred to in the account of the glass now in the Lady Chapel. There have been besides many recent benefactions, including a valuable set of drawings, by herself, of most of the churches in the county of Stafford, left by Mrs Moore, the widow of the Archdeacon of Stafford. There is also in the library a fine old picture of the Duchess of Somerset, as well as an engraving from Sir Joshua Reynolds' picture of Dr Johnson.

Among the most valuable manuscripts and books in the library are the "Gospels of St. Chad," of which more immediately; a fine folio manuscript, on vellum, of Chaucer's "Canterbury Tales," but without the doubtful Ploughman's Tale; the initial letters, especially those at the commencement of each tale, being richly coloured and gilt; the "Valor Ecclesiasticus of Pope Nicholas IV."—this is an account taken of the value of ecclesiastical property in the time of Edward I., from which the tithe granted to the Pope could be ascertained.

Other notable volumes are, "Dives and Pauper," a MS. treatise on the Decalogue—this treatise was one of the earliest

books printed in England ; " Orders generally to be observed of
the whole household of the prince his highness," a large folio,
marked with the sign-manual of King Charles I. at every ordin-
ance ; and a collection of recipes by Sir John Floyer, physician
to Charles II. There is also a volume of MSS. already often
referred to, superscribed, "*Cantaria Sancti Blasii ; Ordi-
natio Majistri Thomæ Heywood decani Eccles. Lich de et super
Cantaria Jesu et Sancta Anne in parte boreai eccles. Lich et de
pensione Capellani ibidem perpetuo celebaturi et aliis articulis,
etc.*" Besides these, there are many rare Bibles :—Cranmer's
Bible, 1540; the " Breeches " Bible ; the " Vinegar " Bible, and
many others.

THE GOSPELS OF ST. CHAD, IN THE LIBRARY.

But to many the most interesting volume in the library will
be a copy of South's Sermons, published in 1694. It
belonged to Dr Johnson, and was used by him in the com-
pilation of his Dictionary. His method, apparently, was to
put a letter in the margin opposite the word whose particular
use here he intended to quote ; and it is interesting, Sermons
in hand, to test his method with the dictionary. On one page
a " K " in the margin is opposite the word " Key." In the dic-

tionary will be found under "Key" the expected quotation from South, "that every man should keep the key of his own breast."

The most valuable book in the library is the *Textus S. Ceddæ*, generally known as "St. Chad's Gospels." This is written on vellum, and contains the Gospels of St. Matthew and St. Mark, and a small portion of the Gospel of St. Luke. It is undoubtedly an Irish MS., probably about the end of the seventh century. There is a page in the book which, with its tesselated work enclosing a cross, recalls to antiquarians similar work in the famous Irish Book of Kells, and in the Gospels of St. Columba which are preserved at Dublin. The connection of an Irish MS. with St. Chad is not difficult of explanation, since, after being taught by St. Aidan at Lindisfarne, he is supposed to have gone, as so many other earnest priests did at the time, to Ireland, to one of the noted monasteries there. The MS. is in Latin, and, with many remarkable variations, follows closely the *Codex Amiatinus* of St Jerome. But its marginal notes are not the least interesting part of the book ; from these, which are sometimes in Celtic and Anglo-Saxon, and sometimes in Latin, we learn something of its history, which is remarkable. The cathedral of Llandaff seems to have acquired it indirectly in exchange for a horse, and there is a note in Celtic, underneath the record of this transaction, which is witnessed by Aidan; whether or no this is the Northumbrian bishop is not known. Another entry, on the page devoted to a picture of St. Luke, shows that the MS. was still at Llandaff at the end of the ninth century ; but on the first page of all is a faint but legible signature which reads "Kynsy" or "Wynsy Praesul," both names of bishops of Lichfield at the end of the tenth century, so that it had probably arrived at its present home not so far short of a thousand years ago. There are other notes connecting it with Lichfield. All these have been printed many times in the pages of learned publications. It owes its escape at the time of the Civil War to the vigilance of William Higgins, Archdeacon of Derby, who was precentor of the cathedral. He abstracted it and kept it until the troubles were over. It now lies in a glass case in the library, side by side with the beautiful "Canterbury Tales." So marvellous are some of the decorations, that it is no wonder that, in an age more faithful than ours, popular belief declared some of them to be "the work of angels."

CHAPTER IV

THE HISTORY OF THE SEE

AT the present day the diocese of Lichfield consists of almost the whole of the county of Stafford, part of Shropshire, and a small part of Flintshire and of Warwickshire. Originally, in Anglo-Saxon times, when the first bishop was appointed, the see of Lichfield extended over the whole of Mercia—that is, from the Humber and East Anglia on the north and east, to Wales on the west, and the Thames on the south. Since those days the diocese has been at various times divided, and other dioceses formed; Hereford, Lincoln, Ely, Peterborough, Chester, Worcester, Oxford, St Albans, Gloucester, Manchester, Liverpool, and Southwell, have all, in whole or in part, been formed out of what was once the diocese of Lichfield.

Of Lichfield in Roman times practically nothing is known. Situated as it is, at a little distance from the crossing of the great Roman roads, Watling Street and Ryknield Street—at which junction the Roman town of Etocetum (the modern Wall) lay, Lichfield was then probably nothing more than open country. The neighbouring towns have yielded a rich harvest of archæological treasures; but beyond coins of various Roman Emperors, bearing Christian emblems, there is little to show that the Gospel had made its way in this part of England; though, in the cemeteries filled with urns containing the ashes of the dead, there have been found, near Burton-on-Trent and near Derby, skeletons, no doubt of Christians who, according to the rites of their religion, had been buried and not burnt.

To Roman times belongs the legend, which is said to give its name to Lichfield, of the massacre of Christians under Diocletian; in consequence, it is related, the place was called Lyccidfelth, or Licidfield—the field of dead men. This is the derivation most generally accepted at the present day; but some etymologists think that Lichfield means Lakefield, from the quantity of water in the neighbourhood.

It is almost certain that the people of Mercia remained pagan from the Roman epoch, and through all the long wars which were waged between the gradually defeated Britons and the Saxons. Three Saxon kings, all pagans, ruled Mercia; and Christianity, which had taken such firm hold in Northumbria, still had not penetrated to the dark central region of Mercia. Then came Penda the Strong, himself a pagan. "He was not baptised," it was said of him, "and never believed in God." He slew many kings, amongst them being the saintly Oswald, king of Northumbria. One of King Penda's daughters had married Alchfrid, a nephew of Oswald and son to the then King Oswy of Northumbria; and in 652 Penda's son, Peada, became suitor for the hand of one of Oswy's daughters. Peada was then ruling under his father the Middle Angles, and he journeyed to the Northumbrian Court, where he was most hospitably received, in spite of the fact that constant war was being waged between Mercia and Northumbria; but the princess whom he sought was promised him only on condition that he and his people in Mid-Anglia should become Christians. Alchfrid became his teacher; and the beauty of this new faith so seized on him that he declared his willingness to become a Christian whether he might win his princess or not. That same year he was baptised by Finan, the British bishop and head of the Church in Northumbria, and with him all his followers. He returned to his own country, taking with him four priests of the British Church: Cedda, who was afterwards made Bishop of London, and who was the brother of St. Chad, Adda, Betti, and Diuma. These four taught the Gospel to the Mid-Anglians, and even went north among the other Mercians; and it does not appear that Penda, in spite of his paganism, made any opposition.

Notwithstanding these close links between the two kingdoms, in the year 655 Penda with an enormous force invaded Northumbria; he was defeated and killed by Oswy, who now became king of Mercia, but left Peada in his old rule in Mid-Anglia. This was the death-blow of paganism in Mercia; Christianity, which was beginning to take firm hold in Peada's country, spread rapidly, and **Diuma** (656-658) was made bishop of Mercia. This may be said to be the commencement of the see which afterwards was called by the name of Lichfield; but as yet there was no cathedral, nor was any place particularly settled upon as the headquarters of the work which was so enthusiastically carried on. Diuma was a travelling or missionary bishop, and when he died, after a brief rule of two years, the Church in Mercia was an accomplished fact.

Diuma was succeeded by **Creollach** (658-659), who, unlike his predecessor an Irishman, was a Briton; he was appointed by Oswy; but in this same year the Mercians rebelled, Oswy fled, and Creollach fled with him, and finally retired to Iona.

The next bishop was a Saxon abbot named **Trumhere** (659-662), and he was succeeded on his death by **Jaruman** (662-667). Both were appointed by King Wulphere, son of Penda, who had been raised to the Mercian throne by his people; and both were Saxons who had been consecrated in the Northumbrian Church. Jaruman was a most energetic bishop, and he appears to have been sent into Essex to reconvert the people there who had fallen into paganism again; his mission was a success, and Jaruman returned to his own people in Mercia.

It was during Jaruman's episcopate that difficulties arose between the Church in Britain and the Church in Rome. Rome had sent messengers to Britain, and they had been the means of converting a large portion of the south coast and of East Anglia; but there were differences in the two Churches, and one particularly caused much trouble. The Roman Church had always kept Easter Day on a Sunday, but the British Church held this feast on March 14, whatever day of the week it might be. A synod was called at Whitby, and it was decided, mainly through the instrumentality of Wilfrid, the future bishop of York, in favour of the Roman Sunday. In this way, it may be said, began the rule of Rome in the English Church. Shortly after, in 667, Jaruman died, and no successor was appointed for two years. During this time, Theodorus of Tarsus became Archbishop of Canterbury, and to him belongs the credit of making the English Church: before, each kingdom had had its own Church, but Theodore welded them together into one whole, and completed their dependence on the bishop of Rome. Wilfrid was made bishop of York, and St. Chad, who had been consecrated to that see, retired to the abbey at Lastingham, only in the next year, 669, to be reconsecrated as bishop of Mercia by the new Archbishop of Canterbury.

St. Chad or **Ceadda** (669-672) made his seat at Lichfield, and in so doing founded the diocese of Lichfield.

St. Chad, as has been stated before, was the patron saint of Lichfield. What is known of him is principally derived from Bede's "Ecclesiastical History of the English Nation." From this we learn that when not on his missionary travels over the diocese he spent most of his time in prayer, and in meditation on death and supernatural things. His method was to proceed from place to place in his diocese on foot; and there is a story of Theodore taking St. Chad in his arms and lifting him on to a horse which he presented to him. He founded the abbey of Barrow-on-Humber, which King Wulphere endowed with fifty hides of land. His headquarters, as we have said, were at Lichfield, and he built, or finished building, a small church near what is still known as St. Chad's Well, at the eastern end of Stowe Pool.

Like his predecessors' his time was short; only for two years was he allowed to labour at Lichfield. There is a beautiful legend of his death which has been well told by Dean Bickersteth. "A week before his death a sound of angelic melody was heard coming from the south-east, until it reached and filled the little oratory where he was praying. This the good bishop interpreted to be his summons to heaven. The voices, he privately told Ovin, were those of angels. The messenger of death, that 'lovable guest,' was with them. They would come again in seven days and take him with them. About the same time, Egbert, a Northumbrian who had been a fellow-student with St. Chad in an Irish monastery, dreamt that he saw the soul of Cedda, Chad's brother, descending from heaven with a company of angels to take the soul of Chad with him into the heavenly kingdom." As he had fore-told, so he died; but he was not forgotten, and many were the miracles said to have been performed at his shrine. His bones were removed from their first resting-place near Stowe Church into a beautiful shrine in the cathedral, where they remained until the Reformation, when they were taken away, and are now said to be in the Roman Catholic cathedral at Birmingham.

There is another legend concerning St. Chad which has become more closely attached to Peterborough than to

Lichfield, but it must be briefly stated here, as the story appears in some of the decorations of the cathedral. Bede does not mention it, and it has been given in varying forms by different writers. Briefly, the essence of the legend is that Wulphere, the king of Mercia, had killed two of his sons, Wulfade and Rufin, on account of their having been baptised by St. Chad. Each of these young princes had been hunting in the forest when he came across a hart with a rope round its neck. The prince gave chase, and the hart led him to St. Chad, who, having prayed with him, baptised him. This happened to both Wulfade and Rufin separately. Then Wulphere in his anger slew them. Afterwards he repented, and setting out to St. Chad, was led there by the same hart, and found the saint at prayer, with his cloak hanging on a sunbeam. Wulphere was absolved on condition that he should expiate his crime by founding churches and monasteries all over his kingdom. Lichfield is said to have been one of these churches, and Peterborough one of these monasteries. Many churches have been dedicated to St. Chad, especially in the Midlands, and in the east of London there was a well known as St. Chad's Well, where miracles were performed; and it was noted for its medicinal waters up to quite recent times. A large district in east London is still called after St. Chad's Well in the corrupted form of Shadwell.

The next bishop was **Winfrid** (672-675), the abbot of St. Chad's Abbey at Barrow-on-Humber; but in the year that he was appointed a church council was held by Theodore, at which it was decided to split up some of the dioceses. Lichfield being one of the largest, would have been divided at once, but Winfrid, whether for his own sake or at the instigation of King Wulphere, resisted, and the diocese remained unchanged until Wulphere died, when in 675, Winfrid, still remaining opposed to the scheme, was deprived. He subsequently was murdered on his way to Rome.

The new bishop was **Saxwulf** (675-691), abbot of Peterborough, and the work of cutting up the diocese was begun. The sees of Hereford and Worcester were made. Lincolnshire was taken from the diocese, and the Middle Angles became the see of Leicester. However, Lichfield still remained an enormous diocese, and when Saxwulf died he was bishop of both Lichfield and Leicester. He was

succeeded by **Hedda** (691-721), who is said to have determined the site of the present cathedral by building a church
there.   However, nothing remains of this cathedral, but it
is always supposed that Hedda brought St. Chad's bones from
Stowe Church and deposited them here.   The cathedral was
dedicated to St. Peter.

Hedda and his successor, **Aldwin** (721-737), were bishops
of both Lichfield and Leicester.   They were followed at
Lichfield by **Witta** (737-752), and the connection with
Leicester ceased.   In 756 Offa, the greatest of the Mercian
kings, ascended the throne.   Offa added a part of Shropshire
to the diocese, which from this time remained the same in extent down to the Reformation.   Here followed three bishops—
Hemele (752-764), **Cuthred** (765-768), and **Berthum** (768-
779)—of whom little is known ; and then came **Higbert** or
Hygeberht (785-801), who holds a remarkable position in the
history of the diocese.   Offa had by this time advanced himself
into the leading position in England ; and so great was his
power that Charlemagne called him emperor of the west, keeping for himself the title of emperor of the east.   But Offa was
first of all king of Mercia, and it did not please him to think
that his bishops were subordinate to an archbishop who lived
in one of his subject states ; and so he determined "to
humble Canterbury and exalt Lichfield."   He began by con-
fiscating all the property of Canterbury situated in Mercia,
and then he appealed to the Pope that the bishop of Lichfield should be made an archbishop.   The Pope assented,
a council held at Chelsea in 785 also agreed, and Higbert,
the new bishop, became archbishop, with the bishoprics of
Worcester, Leicester, Lincoln, and Hereford, parts of the
old diocese of Mercia, as well as Elmham and Dunwich, to
make up his province.   Offa died in 796, and immediately a
stir was made to restore Canterbury to its old dignity.   The
negotiations were long, but in 802 Pope Leo decided in
favour of Canterbury, and the council of Cloveshoe in 803
formally annulled the metropolitan dignity of Lichfield.
Aldulf (801-812), who had succeeded Higbert as archbishop, became bishop, but took precedence after Canterbury
over all the other bishoprics, and **Herewin** (812-818) on his
appointment submitted to Canterbury.

Shortly afterwards **Æthelwald** (818-828) organised the

bishopric upon the basis of its present constitution. Churches were springing up all over the diocese, with their own clergy, and so, although the church at Lichfield remained the head-quarters of the diocese, yet the clergy attached to it were no longer to be responsible for the ministrations of the whole diocese, but were to confine themselves to the estates of the bishop and the cathedral, where they were to dwell under canons or rules. It is possible that from this time the cathedral clergy became known as canons.

Then comes the period of the invasion by the Danes, whereby the country was devastated and the rich abbeys were destroyed. Peterborough, Crowland, and Ely, "went up in flames"; the enemy advanced along the Trent, and levelled to the ground the famous monastery of Repton—the Walhalla of Mercia—where countless kings and princes had been buried. What happened at Lichfield is not known, but many bishops succeeded one another, of whose consecration, in some cases, the dates are so doubtful that it is not worth while to give them. Their names are :—**Hunbert**, 828 ; **Kynebert** ; **Tunfrith** ; **Ella** ; **Algar**, 941 ; **Kinsy**, 949 ; **Winsy**, 964 ; **Elfege**, 973 ; **Godwin**, 1004 ; **Leofgar**, 1020 ; **Brithmar**, 1026 ; and **Wulsy**, 1039 ; but little is known of them, though these two centuries are far from being unimportant in the history of the diocese.

Probably the destruction of the royal abbeys caused the building of numerous parish churches during this period, and of the collegiate churches which were planted in the principal centres of the population. The former were mostly endowed with lands or tithes to support the parish clergy, or to recompense the canons who should attend the church, in which latter case the tithes were probably "appropriated" to the cathedral.

So the system developed until about the year 1000, when began, in Mercia, a new age of monasteries, not like the old royal abbeys which had mostly been destroyed, but houses that were filled with monks or nuns of the Benedictine order. These competed with the secular clergy in appropriating the endowments of the churches, and a jealousy began between the two systems which blazed continually, with greater or less heat, until the final overthrow of the monasteries by Henry VIII. at the beginning of the sixteenth century.

Early in the eleventh century was founded, at Coventry, the

Benedictine abbey which had so great a share in the history of the diocese. Its founder, Earl Leofric, was the husband of the beautiful Godiva whose ride through the town made Coventry free from tolls.

> "I, Luriche, for love of thee,
> Doe make Coventre toll-free,"

are the old words. She induced her husband to found and endow the abbey with its twenty-four monks ; she herself contributed her gold and silver, and the monastery became so wealthy that "the walls seemed almost too strait to hold it all."

Leofwin, bishop of Lichfield (1054-1066), was made the first abbot of Coventry ; he died in the year of the Conquest, and was the last Saxon bishop : henceforth a new order of men was to rule the Church in England.

No doubt Lichfield owed to its insignificance as a city the immunity which it again enjoyed while all the neighbouring country was being pillaged. William appointed his own chaplain, **Peter** (1072-1084), as bishop, and here, no doubt, he lived until 1075, when, at the synod of London, it was decided that the seats of the bishops should be in the larger towns and not in the villages. So to the town of Chester, where there were about 400 or 500 houses, the bishop's seat was moved.

It is interesting to find in " Domesday Book " mention of the extraordinarily heavy fines payable to the bishop at Chester for such offences as the following :—" If any free man does work on a holy day, the bishop has a forfeit of eight shillings. A slave or maidservant so transgressing pays four shillings. A merchant coming into the city and carrying a stall shall pay to the bishop four shillings if he take it down between the ninth hour of the Sabbath and Monday without licence from the bishop's officer."

Following Peter came **Robert de Lymesey** (1087-1117), who, after waiting a short time, obtained papal leave to remove his seat to Coventry, the barony of which he bought from the king; and so he became both bishop and abbot, and for about a century his successors united the two offices. This arrangement was not at all to the taste of the monks, and constant quarrels occurred. Robert de Lymesey is said to have rifled the place; some contend, for the sake of the cathedral at Lichfield, but others, in order to prosecute the suit at Rome in which he was involved with the monks.

The next bishop was **Robert Peche** (1121-1126), and then came **Roger de Clinton** (1129-1148); he was known as the soldier-bishop, and was certainly a strong man, whatever his reputation may have been in other ways. At Lichfield, he was a reformer who did much good to the place. The five canons he found there were dependent for their support on the bishop, and he seems to have settled property on the cathedral to support them. He also added a number of prebendaries, or non-resident canons, who were to be members of the chapter, and were to enjoy a stall in the choir; and to each stall a small estate or prebend was attached. Many other things he did; but, principally, he is supposed to have built the Norman cathedral, and to have fortified the close.

Bishop Roger seems to have been also a great supporter of the Cistercian monks, who appeared in the neighbourhood about this time, and for whom he built an abbey in the diocese at Buildwas, not very far from Shrewsbury. Then, being a soldier as well as a bishop, he started for the East, and died, after fighting in the Crusades, at Antioch in 1148.

Ever since the Conquest the struggles in the Church had been growing sharper. There is no room for a full discussion of these quarrels, but, briefly, it may be said that they arose largely from a desire on the part of the monks and the collegiate churches to shake off the power of the bishops. In doing this it had been necessary to appeal more and more to the Pope, and in consequence the Pope was gradually increasing his power in England, to the detriment not only of the bishops, but also of the king. On the death of Bishop Clinton, Stephen, instead of appointing a successor himself, as had been the custom of the king on previous occasions, found it necessary to depute his authority to a joint council of the monks of Coventry and the canons of Lichfield and Chester. They met at Leicester, and the monks by themselves appointed **Walter Durdent** (1149-1159), prior of Canterbury. The canons would not admit this election, although the new nominee had been precentor at Lichfield; they appealed to Rome, and— how the result came about is not clear, but indeed is a matter of dispute—Durdent was consecrated at Canterbury. He was enthroned at Coventry, but was barred out of Lichfield, where he commenced his rule by excommunicating the canons. But Durdent, being now a bishop, soon drew the canons to his side, and it was with Coventry that the differences continued. He and the prior were summoned to Rome, where it was settled that the bishop should keep the abbey as a monastic cathedral, but that the prior should in the future have the first voice in the election of bishops.

Durdent died at Rome, and was succeeded by **Richard Peche** (1161-1182), son of Robert Peche—for the clergy of that day often married—who seems to have secured the suffrages of both sets of electors. He retired just before his end to the priory of St Thomas, near Stafford, which he had founded in 1180 in memory of Thomas à Becket, who had been murdered ten years previously. He was one of those who had consecrated the archbishop a few years before, and he joined in the popular indignation which ended in the canonisation of the victim. About this time the diocese was permanently divided into the archdeaconries of Derby, Stafford, Chester, and Coventry.

The next bishop was **Gerard Puella** (1183), a celebrated authority on ecclesiastical and canon law. Lichfield refused to admit him, and he died soon after his consecration.

The next bishop was **Hugh de Nonant** or Nunant (1184-1199); his intense hatred of the monks led to terrible disturbances at Coventry. Soon after his consecration he exasperated the monks so greatly that they beat him, and Nonant, with the wounds upon him, hurried to the king, and obtained his consent—some say by purchase—to the monks being turned out. This was done, and secular canons instituted in their place. During the absence of King Richard at the Crusades, Nonant appears to have identified himself too much with the cause of Prince John. This brought about his ruin; for, being suspected by Richard on his return from captivity of participation in the plots against the crown, he was deprived of his bishopric, which in course of time, however, he was allowed to buy back for 5000 marks. He lived not only to see the monks restored to Coventry by the Pope, but also to repent of his harshness to monastical institutions. He died on his way to Rome, and was buried among the monks of Caen.

The next election revived the bitterness between Coventry and Lichfield, a bitterness accentuated by the political adherence of the two parties, Coventry being on King Richard's side,

Lichfield for Prince John. Under these circumstances, the canons had not even been called to the ceremony of election, and Coventry's candidate, **Geoffry de Muschamp** (1198-1208), was elected. But the greatest difficulty of all arose at the election of the next bishop. John was now king, and Lichfield in favour. The monks chose their prior, but John would not allow his consecration; then came a series of proposals, to none of which could king, monks, and canons all three assent, but finally, at the intercession of Pandulf, the Pope's legate, they all agreed on **William de Cornhull** (1215-1223). Thomas of Chesterfield tells us that this bishop conferred the right upon the chapter of electing their own dean.

The next bishop, **Alexander de Stavenby** (1224-1238), was appointed by the Pope, on the appeal to him of both parties, who were still unable to agree. He built the friary in Lich-field, and dedicated it to St. Francis, the founder of the Friar Minors, which order he first introduced into the diocese.

The high position of Stavenby in the councils of the realm make him an important personality among the bishops of the diocese. He died in 1238; and it might have been expected that a successor would have been appointed without difficulty, for during his rule it had been agreed that Coventry and Lichfield should appoint to the vacant bishopric alternately. Coventry appointed William de Raleigh, but he accepted Norwich in preference, and then the monks claimed to appoint again, but the canons would not allow this, and appointed their dean, William of Manchester, who, however, stood aside when the monks suggested Nicholas de Farnham, and he was too modest to accept the office. Then **Hugh de Patteshull** (1239-1241) was chosen at the king's desire. He was Treasurer of England and a native of the diocese; he seems to have followed in the steps of his predecessor, and it is said that he made new regulations as to the manner of the cathedral services. He died only eighteen months after his appointment, and a fresh trouble arose over the election of a successor; but the Pope intervened without asking permission of the king, and, under the advice of Grosseteste, the famous bishop of Lincoln, appointed **Roger de Weseham** (1245-1256), the dean of the cathedral. The king in his anger seized the endowments of the see, and Weseham began his work amid great difficulties, but finally Henry restored the endowments, and allowed Weseham to prosecute his salutary re-organisation of the clergy. Weseham retired in 1256, and died shortly after. It is doubtful if the monument in the south aisle, generally known as that of Bishop Patteshull, is not in reality that of Bishop Weseham.

There was no contention over the election of the next bishop, **Roger de Molend** or Meyland (1256-1295). He was a natural son of the Earl of Salisbury, William Longespée, and so nephew to King Henry III. His was not an admirable role, the most remarkable event being his attempt, *vi et armis*, to obtain admittance to the Royal Free Chapel of St. Mary at Stafford. Both sides refused to plead at the Assizes, but it was finally decided that the bishop should be allowed the use of the free chapels in Derby and Stafford, but should have no disciplinary powers over their clergy. Afterwards he seems to have neglected his diocese, and the scandalous and avaricious conduct of the clergy, which the last two bishops had controlled, now became so intense that in 1282 Archbishop Peckham had to interfere, and Roger was forced to come into residence. Soon after it was found necessary to find him a coadjutor, who was to advise him in all official acts. Incompetent as he was as a bishop, the diocese obtained several remarkable benefits during his rule. The king gave Cannock Chase to the see, and the west front of the cathedral was begun. It may well be that in his travels he had acquired a love of beauty he would not have acquired at home, and that we owe to him the conception of this beautiful feature of the cathedral. The money it must have cost, too, could only have been found by one whose princely rank enabled him to obtain money with some ease. In London also he left his mark, unhappily now entirely obliterated. Where Somerset House now stands he erected his palace, next to the palace of his brother Bishop of Worcester. It was a beautiful mansion, but the site was too valuable to permit of it belonging to any one but the king when Henry VIII. graced the throne.

About this time the archdeaconry of Stafford was occupied by Thomas de Cantilupe, afterwards Bishop of Hereford. The story of his life belongs to the account of that diocese, but such a man must have had great influence on his archdeaconry.

The next bishop was **Walter de Langton** (1296-1321), Treasurer of England, and friend to King Edward I.

He was chosen unanimously by both parties. At first his political duties claimed him, and brought him into collision with the Prince of Wales, who, as soon as he had ascended the throne as Edward II., threw him into prison. There he does not seem to have remained long, and when Piers Gaveston, the king's favourite, was beheaded in 1312, he was restored to his former treasurership. Langton is principally remembered in connection with the see as having founded the Lady Chapel and built the Bishop's Palace, for so long a splendid monument to his memory in the north-east corner of the close. He rebuilt also Eccleshall and Haywood Manor houses, and walled the close for "the honour of God, the dignity of the cathedral, and the bodies of the saints there reposing, and also for security and quiet of the canons." This last a mistaken work, as we who live after the event are well able to judge. He also bridged the cathedral pool, and made a magnificent shrine for St. Chad's bones. Langton died in 1321 in London, and was carried to Lichfield, where he was buried with much ceremony. His bones were removed into the Lady Chapel when it was finished during the rule of the next bishop, and a sumptuous monument placed over them. The mutilated remains of this monument can be seen in the south choir aisle to this day.

His successor, **Roger de Norbury** or Northbury (1322-1359), was appointed by the Pope, as the two chapters had not agreed once more. His was a long rule, nearly forty years, and filled with good for the see. The registers of both Langton and Norbury are both still in existence among the muniments of the cathedral, and from them we know much of the life of a bishop of this time. Every kind of evil seems to have come under the notice of the bishop—whose power of inducing those who had done wrong to repent and do right was the direct outcome of the terrible threat of excommunication which he was able to wield. Lichfield had constantly during the later reigns been the scene of royal festivities, and after the battle of Crecy Edward III. held his Court here, and there were tournaments and banquets at which the flower of English chivalry assisted. It is said by some that here occurred the famous incident of the garter which led to the institution of the order of that name.

At any rate, Uttoxeter was appropriated to the chapel of the garter.

About this time, too, the cathedral must have been finished; now, too, was the terrible visitation of the black death, that most deadly of all plagues, which is said to have cut off one half of the whole population of the realm. Whether the fear of it, or the occasion of the completion of the cathedral, caused the chapter to set their house in order, certain it is that we have, in the discovery of the sacrist's roll of 1346, a kind of inventory of the valuables of the cathedral at this time; these are set out in the part devoted to the cathedral. Thomas of Chesterfield, the early historian of the diocese, whose work is printed in Wharton's *Anglia Sacra*, and on whom all later writers on the subject have had largely to rely, lived at this time, and brought down his "chronicle" to 1348, one of the years of the black death.

Roger de Stretton (1360-1386), an absolutely uneducated man, succeeded Langton; then came **Walter Skirlaw** (1386) and **Richard Scrope** (1386-1396), but the former, between his consecration and his enthronement, was translated to Bath and Wells, from whence he went to Durham, and the latter, though distinguished in English history, is more noted as Archbishop of York. Next came Bishop **John Burghill** (1398-1414), a barefooted Black Friar, who gained a reputation for asceticism, and left his worldly goods to the church. Richard II. was present at the enthronement of these two last bishops. They were followed by **John Catterick** (1415-1419).

In 1419, **William Heyworth** (1419-1447), the abbot of St. Albans, became bishop. An important question was settled in his time—viz. the bishop's position in the cathedral. At his suggestion, it was arranged that he should give notice to the dean when he intended a visitation: the chapter should be summoned, and they should conduct him to the high altar and there leave him to stand or kneel alone in prayer. Afterwards they were to conduct him to the chapter-house, where he might inquire into the title and conduct of the canons; the other cathedral clergy were to be entirely subject to the dean and chapter. His rule saw also the beginnings of the collegiate church of Manchester, which so long after was to become the cathedral of the new diocese to be carved out of our see.

It is unnecessary to more than mention the names of bishops

who succeeded about this time : they are—**William Booth** (1447-1450), **Nicholas Cloose** (1452), **Reginald Bolars** (1453-1459). **John Halse** (1459-1492) was called on to give shelter to Queen Margaret after the battle of Bloreheath.

At the end of the fifteenth century there is another political bishop. This was **William Smyth** (1492-1496). He, like several of his successors, was President of Wales, and he was also the founder of Brasenose College, Oxford. Next comes **John Arundel** (1496-1503), and then comes **Geoffry Blythe**, whose rule, commencing in 1503, lasts until 1531, the year when Henry required the clergy to acknowledge him as supreme head of the Church. This period of the dark days before the Reformation must have been one of great difficulty for the bishops, but Blythe seems to have been very popular at Lichfield ; he made several attempts to stamp out Lollardism, and has earned for himself an unenviable niche in the house of fame by his inclusion in Fox's "Book of Martyrs" for his holding of the "Court of Heresy." One martyr (a woman) was burned at Coventry, and others were tried and acquitted or condemned to less horrible punishments. On the whole, Blythe seems to have been as gentle as the times would allow him to be. He died in 1531, and escaped the storm which was now to burst. When it had cleared away, many of the old religious landmarks had disappeared ; Lichfield Cathedral had lost her sister minster, and had been shorn of much that it valued and was beautiful.

After an interval, **Rowland Lee** (1534-1543) was appointed. He had been chaplain to the king, and it was he who officiated at the private marriage of Henry and Anne Boleyn ; he was rewarded with the bishopric of Lichfield and Coventry, and was made President of Wales, in which latter appointment he was said to have ruled so wisely that we owe to him the kindly feelings which have ever since existed between the two countries. This work must have kept him much away from the diocese, and it was superintended by two suffragans ; but we have it on record that he did his best to save something for the diocese from the wreck of the Reformation ; how little he was able to do we shall now see. He also issued to the clergy a set of injunctions, in which the new teaching and ideas are set forth, "that the King's Majesty is only Supreme Head under Chryst in Erthe of this his Churche of England"; that every parish priest shall provide for his church a " Boke of the hole Byble both in Latin and alsoe in Englishe, and lay the same in the Quiere for every man that will loke and read therein "; and other injunctions on prayers and preaching and behaviour, which are not, like the first two, new and startling, but are reminiscences of the ordinances and manners of the past.

Bishop Lee, who had failed in his efforts to save the cathedral church of Coventry, also exerted himself on behalf of the shrine of St. Chad, and succeeded so well that, though the shrine was rifled of its jewels and precious metals, they were granted to the uses of the cathedral, instead of finding their way into the coffers of the king. The ashes of the saint were stolen by one of the prebendaries. Soon after, the collegiate churches were confiscated, and the diocese, like other dioceses, found itself stripped of all its finest churches. The royal chapels of Stafford, Shrewsbury, Chester, Bridgenorth, Derby, and Penkridge all went; and throughout the country, for want of the endowments which had been confiscated, churches and chapels were falling into ruin.

Henry seems to have had ideas of using some of the money thus obtained for ecclesiastical purposes, but his own needs did not permit him to do much. The bishopric of Shrewsbury, which he had planned, came to nothing, though a suffragan with that title was appointed ; but at Chester the abbey of St. Werburgh became a cathedral church when, in 1541, the see of Chester was founded, and Cheshire and Lancashire were taken from Lichfield to form the new diocese.

Richard Sampson (1543-1553), dean of the cathedral, succeeded Lee as bishop, and died early in Mary's reign. His successor, **Ralph Bane** (1554-1558), lighted the fires in the diocese, and many perished at his hands. He was a bishop after Mary's heart, and sat with Tonstall and Bonner in the inquisitions which disgraced the reign. He resigned on the advent of Elizabeth. And then another kind of persecution commenced ; this time it was the Papists who suffered, and many were done to death in the diocese.

Following Bane came **Thomas Bentham** (1560-1579), and **William Overton** (1580-1609); then **George Abbott** was bishop in 1609, and in one year was promoted to Canterbury, where he preceded Laud, whose life-long opponent he was.

Then came **Richard Neill** (1610-1614), who was dean of West-minster as well, and earned an ignoble reputation by burning a Papist named Wightman, at Lichfield. He was consecrated to Rochester in 1608, and translated successively to Lichfield, 1610; Lincoln, 1614; Durham, 1617; Winchester, 1628; and York, 1632. **John Overall** (1614-1618) wrote that part of the " Church Catechism " which explains the sacraments; he after-wards went to Norwich. **Thomas Morton** (1619-1632) came from Chester; he was one of the most learned bishops of the time, and a noted advocate of the Church of England principles.

Robert Wright (1632-1644) was a supporter of Laud; under him the cathedral service became again something like that of the time of Bishop Patteshull. He was one of the twelve bishops who were impeached by the Long Parliament in 1641, and, though an old man, pleaded his cause at the bar of the House of Commons. He was still bishop when the Civil War broke out; and during the famous siege of Lichfield he was shut up in his castle at Eccleshall, where he died while it was being defended against the Parliamentarians. His successor, **Accepted Frewen,** president of Magdalen College, Oxford, was appointed by the king, and consecrated in the chapel of his college; but, having neither cathedral, revenues, nor power, he retired into Kent, until in 1660 he became Archbishop of York.

John Hacket (1661-1671) was appointed to the see by Charles II., and decided that its title should be altered from " Coventry and Lichfield " to "Lichfield and Coventry"; partly, no doubt, because the cathedral was here, and partly because in the late troubles Lichfield had been loyal to the Crown, and Coventry had not. His great work was the restoration of the cathedral from its ruins, and the re-organisation of the diocese. He had had a distinguished record, and was one of the sub-committee in 1640 appointed to try and settle the vexed questions in the Church, and as such he made an eloquent speech at the bar of the House of Commons. Later he continued the use of the liturgy in his church of St. Andrew, Holborn, after it had been forbidden, and when the officer and soldiers were sent to arrest him and ordered him to desist on pain of instant death, he answered: "Soldier, I am doing my duty, do you do yours," and continued the service. Surely a man pre-eminently fitted for the work of re-organisation he was to do at Lichfield; and the king got the credit from the clergy of having the old "apostolic spirit of discerning," so greatly was he to their minds. He must have been a wit too, for, when the bishopric was offered to him, he remarked that he would rather that in future times people should ask why Dr Hacket was not a bishop, than why he was. He is also said to have entreated the gentleman who had declared that hell was paved with bishops' skulls to tread lightly over his.

Hacket's dean cannot have confirmed the clergy in their opinion of Charles, whose appointment to the post he had purchased ; so bad was he that the bishop excommunicated him, and the sentence was even read in the cathedral while he was there, but he heeded it not. The chapter loathed him, but apparently the king's feelings were different, for at Hacket's death he was appointed to succeed him. So **Thomas Wood** (1671-1692) became bishop, and was the worst the see ever had : he lived much away from the diocese. Lancelot Addison, the father of the famous Joseph Addison, was dean in his time. William III., staying a night at the deanery, was attracted to the genial essayist early ; and we may imagine that he must have been greatly influenced by that part of his life spent within the cathedral close.

The next bishop was **William Lloyd** (1692-1699): he came from St. Asaph, and went to Worcester. While bishop of St. Asaph he was one of the seven bishops who were sent to the Tower in 1688. **John Hough** (1699-1717) came next; he also had crossed the path of James II., for he had been elected President of Magdalen over the head of James's nominee, but James had proved the stronger at the time, and he was ejected, only to be reinstated by the frightened king soon after. At the Revolution he was made bishop of Oxford, whence he was translated hither ; he afterwards refused the primacy.

The next two bishops—**Edward Chandler** (1717-1730) and **Richard Smallbroke** (1730-1749)—were distinguished defenders of Christianity against the infidelity of the time. Their controversial writings are numerous and well known.

The next bishop, **Frederick Cornwallis** (1749-1768), afterwards became Archbishop of Canterbury. Then came **John Egerton** (1768-1771), from Bangor, and went to Durham ; **Brownlow North** (1771-1774), who was translated to Worcester, and thence to Winchester ; **Richard Hurd** (1774-1781), who also went to Worcester ; **James**

Cornwallis (1781-1824), and **Henry Ryder** (1824-1836), who came from Gloucester. He succeeded in founding many new churches and immensely increasing the membership of the Church in the diocese. His successor, **Samuel Butler** (1836-1843), went on with this work. It was in his time that the archdeaconry of Coventry was taken from the diocese and added to Worcester. The title of the see now becomes Lichfield only; Coventry, which at one time held the premier place in the title, and then the second, now slips out altogether.

Ten years later the deanery of Bridgenorth was allotted to Hereford, and in the same year all peculiar and exempt jurisdiction was abolished, so that the archdeacons had power to visit every church in the diocese; the number of canons of Lichfield was reduced from six to four.

In the meantime **James Bowstead** (1840-1843) and **John Lonsdale** (1843-1867) became bishops. The latter was one of the greatest bishops the diocese has had, and his work, like that of Ryder, lives in the increased power of the Church in the diocese. He was succeeded by another great bishop, **George Augustus Selwyn,** who, as bishop of New Zealand, had organised the Church in those islands.

The next bishop, **William Dalrymple Maclagan** (1878-1891), is now Archbishop of York. It was during his rule, in 1884, that the new diocese of Southwell was formed and Derbyshire was taken from Lichfield.

The present bishop is the Hon. **Augustus Legge.**

Photochrom Co. Ltd., Photo.]

MONUMENT TO DR JOHNSON IN THE
MARKET-PLACE.

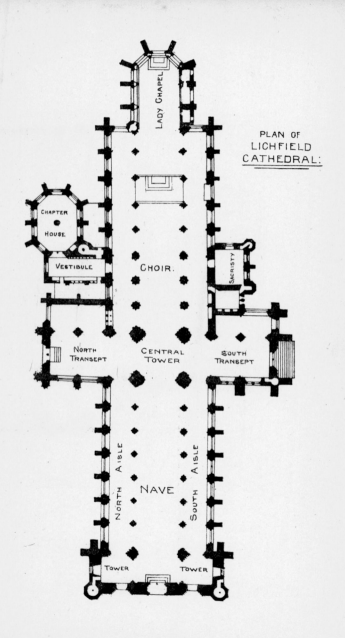

PLAN OF
LICHFIELD
CATHEDRAL:

LADY CHAPEL

CHAPTER
HOUSE

VESTIBULE

CHOIR.

SACRISTY

NORTH
TRANSEPT

CENTRAL
TOWER

SOUTH
TRANSEPT

NORTH AISLE

SOUTH AISLE

NAVE

TOWER

TOWER

Bell's Cathedral Series.

EDITED BY

GLEESON WHITE and E. F. STRANGE.

In specially designed cloth cover, crown 8vo, 1s. 6d. each.

Now Ready.

CANTERBURY. By HARTLEY WITHERS. 2nd Edition, revised. 36 Illustrations.

SALISBURY. By GLEESON WHITE. 2nd Edition, revised. 50 Illustrations.

CHESTER. By CHARLES HIATT. 24 Illustrations.

ROCHESTER. By G. H. PALMER, B.A. 38 Illustrations.

OXFORD. By Rev. PERCY DEARMER, M.A. 34 Illustrations.

EXETER. By PERCY ADDLESHAW, B.A. 35 Illustrations.

PETERBOROUGH. By Rev. W. D. SWEETING. 51 Illustrations.

WINCHESTER. By P. W. SERGEANT. 50 Illustrations.

NORWICH. By C. H. B. QUENNELL. 38 Illustrations.

LICHFIELD. By A. B. CLIFTON. 42 Illustrations.

HEREFORD. By A. HUGH FISHER. 34 Illustrations.

Preparing.

LINCOLN. By A. B. KENDRICK, B.A.	SOUTHWELL. By Rev. ARTHUR DIMOCK.
DURHAM. By J. E. BYGATE.	ELY. By T. D. ATKINSON.
WELLS. By Rev. PERCY DEARMER, M.A.	WORCESTER. By E. F. STRANGE.
ST DAVID'S. By PHILIP ROBSON.	YORK. By A. CLUTTON BROCK, B.A.
CHICHESTER. CARLISLE.	BRISTOL. GLOUCESTER.
ST ALBANS. ST PAUL'S.	RIPON.

Uniform with the above Series.

BEVERLEY MINSTER. By CHARLES HIATT. [*Preparing.*

Opinions of the Press.

"For the purpose at which they aim they are admirably done, and there are few visitants to any of our noble shrines who will not enjoy their visit the better for being furnished with one of these delightful books, which can be slipped into the pocket and carried with ease, and is yet distinct and legible. . . . A volume such as that on Canterbury is exactly what we want, and on our next visit we hope to have it with us. It is thoroughly helpful, and the views of the fair city and its noble cathedral are beautiful. Both volumes, moreover, will serve more than a temporary purpose, and are trustworthy as well as delightful."—*Notes and Queries.*

"We have so frequently in these columns urged the want of cheap, well-illustrated, and well-written handbooks to our cathedrals, to take the place of the out-of-date publications of local booksellers, that we are glad to hear that they have been taken in hand by Messrs George Bell and Sons."—*St James's Gazette.*

"Visitors to the cathedral cities of England must often have felt the need of some work dealing with the history and antiquities of the city itself, and the architecture and associations of the cathedral, more portable than the elaborate monographs which have been devoted to some of them, more scholarly and satisfying than the average local guide-book, and more copious than the section devoted to them in the general guide-book of the county or district. Such a legitimate need the 'Cathedral Series' now being issued by Messrs George Bell & Sons, under the editorship of Mr Gleeson White and Mr E. F. Strange, seems well calculated to supply. The volumes are handy in size, moderate in price, well illustrated, and written in a scholarly spirit. The history of cathedral and city is intelligently set forth and accompanied by a descriptive survey of the building in all its detail. The illustrations are copious and well selected, and the series bids fair to become an indispensable companion to the cathedral tourist in England."—*Times*.

"They are nicely produced in good type, on good paper, and contain numerous illustrations, are well written, and very cheap. We should imagine architects and students of architecture will be sure to buy the series as they appear, for they contain in brief much valuable information." —*British Architect*.

"Half the charm of this little book on Canterbury springs from the writer's recognition of the historical association of so majestic a building with the fortunes, destinies, and habits of the English people. . . . One admirable feature of the book is its artistic illustrations. They are both lavish and satisfactory—even when regarded with critical eyes."— *Speaker*.

"Every aspect of Salisbury is passed in swift, picturesque survey in this charming little volume, and the illustrations in this case also heighten perceptibly the romantic appeal of an unconventional but scholarly guide-book."—*Speaker*.

"There is likely to be a large demand for these attractive handbooks." —*Globe*.

"Bell's 'Cathedral Series,' so admirably edited, is more than a description of the various English cathedrals. It will be a valuable historical record, and a work of much service also to the architect. The illustrations are well selected, and in many cases not mere bald architectural drawings but reproductions of exquisite stone fancies, touched in their treatment by fancy and guided by art."—*Star*.

"Each of them contains exactly that amount of information which the intelligent visitor, who is not a specialist, will wish to have. The disposition of the various parts is judiciously proportioned, and the style is very readable. The illustrations supply a further important feature ; they are both numerous and good. A series which cannot fail to be welcomed by all who are interested in the ecclesiastical buildings of England."— *Glasgow Herald*.

"Those who, either for purposes of professional study or for a cultured recreation, find it expedient to 'do' the English cathedrals will welcome the beginning of Bell's 'Cathedral Series.' This set of books is an attempt to consult, more closely, and in greater detail than the usual guide-books do, the needs of visitors to the cathedral towns. The series cannot but prove markedly successful. In each book a business-like description is given of the fabric of the church to which the volume relates, and an interesting history of the relative diocese. The books are plentifully illustrated, and are thus made attractive as well as instructive. They cannot but prove welcome to all classes of readers interested either in English Church history or in ecclesiastical architecture."—*Scotsman*.

"A set of little books which may be described as very useful, very pretty, and very cheap . . . . and alike in the letterpress, the illustrations, and the remarkably choice binding, they are ideal guides."— *Liverpool Daily Post*.

"They have nothing in common with the almost invariably wretched local guides save portability, and their only competitors in the quality and quantity of their contents are very expensive and mostly rare works, each of a size that suggests a packing-case rather than a coat-pocket. The 'Cathedral Series' are important compilations concerning history, architecture, and biography, and quite popular enough for such as take any sincere interest in their subjects."—*Sketch*.

LONDON : GEORGE BELL AND SONS.